WITNESSES
OF THE
MESSIAH

WITNESSES OF THE MESSIAH

On Acts of the Apostles 1-15

Stephen Pimentel

With a Foreword by Tim Gray

EMMAUS ROAD
PUBLISHING
Steubenville, Ohio

Emmaus Road Publishing
827 North Fourth Street
Steubenville, Ohio 43952

Library of Congress Control Number: 2002100609
ISBN 1-931018-12-X

Unless otherwise indicated, Scripture quotations are taken
from the Revised Standard Version, Catholic Edition (RSVCE),
© 1965, 1966 by the Division of Christian Education of the
National Council of the Churches of Christ in the
United States of America. Used by permission.

Excerpts from the English translation of the
Catechism of the Catholic Church for the United States of America
© 1994, United States Catholic Conference, Inc.—Libreria Editrice
Vaticana. English translation of the *Catechism of the Catholic Church:
Modifications from the Editio Typica* © 1997,
United States Catholic Conference, Inc.
—Libreria Editrice Vaticana.

On the cover
Guido Reni, *Saints Peter and Paul*

Cover design and layout by
Beth Hart

Nihil Obstat: Rev. James Dunfee, *Censor Librorum*
Imprimatur: ✠ Gilbert I. Sheldon, D.D., D.Min., Bishop of Steubenville
January 14, 2002

The *Nihil Obstat* and *Imprimatur* are official declarations
that a book or pamphlet is free of doctrinal or moral error.
No implication is contained therein that those who have
granted the *Nihil Obstat* and *Imprimatur* agree with
the contents, opinions, or statements expressed.

To Rachel

*"Lord, will you at this time restore
the kingdom to Israel?"*
—Acts 1:6

CONTENTS

CHAPTER 1
The World of Acts 3
Covenantal History 3; The Abrahamic Promise 4; The Kingdom
of God 5; The People of God 6; Jew and Gentile United 7;
The New Exodus 8; The Wilderness Generation 9; The Last
Days 10; Questions for Discussion 12

CHAPTER 2
Christ the King (Acts 1) 17
The Advance of the Kingdom 17; The Twelve Tribes of Israel 18;
The End of the Earth 19; Coming to the Throne 20; The
Victory of the Gospel 21; The College of the Twelve 22; The
Testimony of the Scriptures 23; Officers of the New Temple 25;
Questions for Discussion 26

CHAPTER 3
The Church of the Last Days (Acts 2:1-21) 29
The Giving of the Law 29; The New Law of the Spirit 31; Israel
Reunited 32; Foreign Tongues 33; Witness in Jerusalem 34; The
Last Days 35; The Gift of the Spirit 37; Apocalyptic Signs 38;
Escape from Jerusalem 39; Questions for Discussion 40

CHAPTER 4
The Preaching of Peter (Acts 2:22-47) 43
David's Prophecy 43; The Right Hand of God 45; Exaltation of
the Messiah 45; Repentance and Baptism 47; The Promise 48;
This Crooked Generation 49; The Church of Jerusalem 50;
Questions for Discussion 51

FOREWORD

The evangelist Luke wrote both the Gospel of Luke and Acts of the Apostles. This means more than the fact that both books share the same literary style, vocabulary, and perspective. They share the same plot. Indeed, Luke begins his sequel to his Gospel by noting how the second work is a continuation of the first, because the life of Jesus is recapitulated in the life of the Church. "In the first book, O Theophilus, I have dealt with all that Jesus began to do and teach" (Acts 1:1). Note the key verb "began," which underscores that the story of Jesus has not ended but rather has surprisingly taken on a new form in the life of the Church.

This is illustrated by the many parallels between the life of Jesus and the lives of the apostles. For example, Luke highlights how Jesus' public ministry began with the visible descent of the Holy Spirit upon Jesus, from which Jesus goes forth anointed in the power of the Holy Spirit (Lk. 3). The apostles, too, begin their ministry with the descent of the Holy Spirit at Pentecost. Thenceforth they, too, do everything by the power of the Spirit. Thus, Pentecost is to the Church what the anointing at the Jordan was to Jesus: the commissioning for mission in the Spirit. The Church in her own life relives the mysteries of the life of Jesus. In other words, through the apostles and the Church, Jesus continues to act and teach.

How can Jesus still be active, given that He is dead (albeit now resurrected)? This is Luke's starting point in Acts. Jesus' Resurrection is more than simply a return of life from death, an escape from mortality in order to vanish into some distant heaven. Rather, His victory over death is followed by a royal Ascension through which He is exalted and enthroned at the right hand of God, from where He sends out His Spirit and begins an active reign. For Luke and the early Christians, Jesus' Ascension was more than an exit; it was an entry into the heavenly throne room from which He directs the course of history and the life of the Church.

The kingship of Christ and the realm of His dominion, which is the Church, are some of the many themes of Acts, which Steve Pimentel writes about with passion, depth, and amazing clarity. Steve elucidates how the Church constitutes the kingdom of God and the fulfillment of God's plan for His people in salvation history. Luke himself has framed his story of Acts with the motif of the kingdom. At the outset of Acts, the apostles ask Jesus if now is the time that He will "restore the kingdom to Israel" (Acts 1:6). The question is answered only indirectly, leaving the reader wondering about the nature of the kingdom and its timing. But as Steve so lucidly argues in this wonderful book, the Church herself is the reconstitution of the kingdom, and it is a kingdom that bursts the old confines of ethnic Israel. The new Israel is fathered by the spiritual patrimony of the twelve apostles, a patrimony that dramatically reconfigures the twelve tribes of Israel. This point is borne out at the very end of Acts, which ends with Paul proclaiming the good news of the "kingdom of God" (Acts 28:31) in the capital of the civilized world, Rome.

Astonishingly, the Gospel that began to be proclaimed in Jerusalem has now reached the very
capital of the Roman Empire, thereby suggesting that
the kingdom of Christ is eclipsing Caesar's kingdom.
Undoubtedly, if Paul's preaching extends the kingdom
as far as Rome, Christ's dominion is already exercised
in the life of the Church. In short, Paul answers the
apostles' question by showing that the time of the
kingdom has already begun, but its borders stretch
out past the limited borders of Israel. The kingdom is
not restored to ethnic Israel, but rather ethnic Israel is
renewed so as to restore all people into the kingdom
of God. Thus the ethnic and geographic limitations
set out in the Old Covenant are transformed into the
limitless boundaries of the New Covenant, which is
universal—that is, Catholic—in scope. This is why
Luke ends his narrative with Paul in Rome, for he
has demonstrated that the actions of the apostles
have fulfilled Jesus' wish that the kingdom of the
New Covenant extend to all peoples and places.
Luke's literary *inclusio* frames his story of the
Church by beginning and ending it with the kingdom
motif (Acts 1:6; 28:31).

Steve Pimentel has done us a great service in pro-
viding such an illuminating guide to the Acts of the
Apostles. His treatment is deeply Catholic. Pimentel
provides a biblical theology that is potent wine, far
from the watered-down treatments that too often
give us a de-theologized treatment of the history of
the early Church in Acts. Pimentel plunges the
reader into the heart of the matter, showing how
the early Church bears witness to the Father's plan
for salvation history. *Witnesses of the Messiah* is that

rare book that can take one into the theological depths of Scripture while at the same time maintaining clarity and an ease of reading that is truly admirable. I am sure that your reading of Pimentel's fine study will inspire you, as it did me, to reread Acts of the Apostles with deeper insight and clarity.

Luke dedicated his two volumes to a man named Theophilus, which means "lover of God." Besides the historical Theophilus, each one of us is invited to be a "Theophilus," a lover of God; and who can help but grow in love for God as he reads about His deeds in the lives of the apostles? So as you read Steve Pimentel's wonderful book on Acts, *Witnesses of the Messiah*, at the same time be sure to read the treasure of the Church's memory, Acts of the Apostles. And after you read them, ponder how Jesus' last words to the apostles now apply to you: "You are witnesses of these things" (Lk. 24:48).

Tim Gray

PREFACE

A note on documentation: In keeping with the popular nature of the work, footnotes throughout the text have been kept to an absolute minimum. Accordingly, I have included footnotes only to those sources that I have drawn on most heavily, and, within each chapter, I have noted only the first citation of a given source.

Abbreviations

Old Testament
Gen./Genesis
Ex./Exodus
Lev./Leviticus
Num./Numbers
Deut./Deuteronomy
Josh./Joshua
Judg./Judges
Ruth/Ruth
1 Sam./1 Samuel
2 Sam./2 Samuel
1 Kings/1 Kings
2 Kings/2 Kings
1 Chron./1 Chronicles
2 Chron./2 Chronicles
Ezra/Ezra
Neh./Nehemiah
Tob./Tobit
Jud./Judith
Esther/Esther
Job/Job
Ps./Psalms
Prov./Proverbs
Eccles./Ecclesiastes
Song/Song of Solomon
Wis./Wisdom
Sir./Sirach (Ecclesiasticus)
Is./Isaiah
Jer./Jeremiah
Lam./Lamentations
Bar./Baruch
Ezek./Ezekiel
Dan./Daniel
Hos./Hosea

Joel/Joel
Amos/Amos
Obad./Obadiah
Jon./Jonah
Mic./Micah
Nahum/Nahum
Hab./Habakkuk
Zeph./Zephaniah
Hag./Haggai
Zech./Zechariah
Mal./Malachi
1 Mac./1 Maccabees
2 Mac./2 Maccabees

New Testament
Mt./Matthew
Mk./Mark
Lk./Luke
Jn./John
Acts/Acts of the Apostles
Rom./Romans
1 Cor./1 Corinthians
2 Cor./2 Corinthians
Gal./Galatians
Eph./Ephesians
Phil./Philippians
Col./Colossians
1 Thess./1 Thessalonians
2 Thess./2 Thessalonians
1 Tim./1 Timothy
2 Tim./2 Timothy
Tit./Titus
Philem./Philemon

Heb./Hebrews
Jas./James
1 Pet./1 Peter
2 Pet./2 Peter
1 Jn./1 John
2 Jn./2 John
3 Jn./3 John
Jude/Jude
Rev./Revelation (Apocalypse)

Catechism of the Catholic Church

Throughout the text, the *Catechism of the Catholic Church* will be cited simply as Catechism.

INTRODUCTION

The Book of Acts is a work of both history and theology, an account of God's self-revelation within the course of human history.[1] Hence, to understand what Luke intended to communicate in Acts, one must set aside the false dichotomy between history and theology. In Luke's biblical theology, history itself is a framework created and governed by God through which He reveals Himself to man. Thus, Acts must be read with a critical realism that seeks to discern the author's intention as recorded in the canonical writing itself (cf. Second Vatican Council, *Dei Verbum*, no. 12). Luke unfolds his narrative of the Holy Spirit's action within the apostolic Church in a manner that gradually reveals the relation between the New Covenant established by Jesus Christ and the covenants of the Old Testament.

Luke's covenantal theology is therefore intrinsically historical in its outlook, focusing as it does on the sequence of covenants by which God has progressively redeemed His people, beginning with the covenants of the Old Testament and culminating in the events that Luke himself records. It has become popular in recent years to insist upon the centrality of covenantal thought in biblical theology, but there has also been a certain hesitance to apply this insight consistently to the interpretation of the

---

[1] N. T. Wright, *The New Testament and the People of God*, Christian Origins and the Question of God, vol. 1 (Minneapolis: Fortress Press, 1992), 383-84.

New Testament. A consistent covenantal theology requires one to confront a number of key questions that will shape one's understanding of Acts. Among these questions are the following:

1. If Jesus inaugurated a New Covenant, did the apostles consider their generation to be living through a transition of covenants?
2. Was the apostles' preaching situated in the context of such a covenantal transition?
3. Did the impending judgment that Jesus insisted would be witnessed by "this generation" (Lk. 11:50-51; 21:32) in fact come to pass in the first century?
4. Did the Roman conquest of Jerusalem and destruction of the Temple have a covenantal significance?

Luke's narrative of the apostles' ministry bears the marks of an affirmative answer to each of these questions.

Within this covenantal framework, Luke sets forth his major themes, emphasizing the sovereign agency of God. From the Ascension onward, Christ reigns from heaven, while from Pentecost onward, the Holy Spirit rules within the Church. God has visited His people and continues to do so, gathering all the nations into the Church. God's salvific plan has been foretold in prophecy and is now being fulfilled, as it necessarily must be (cf. Acts 1:16; 3:21). Luke looks upon the events he describes with a spiritual vision, seeing them as salvific acts of God to be interpreted through the prophetic Scriptures. Acts, to be understood within its historical context, must be read with a grasp of this spiritual vision.

The World of Acts

The book that we call the Acts of the Apostles was written by Luke as a sequel to his Gospel and, like that Gospel, is a work centered on a mission. Whereas the Gospel of Luke describes the mission of Jesus the Messiah, Acts carries forward the narrative by describing the mission of the Holy Spirit working in and through the apostles. Luke depicts the outpouring of the Holy Spirit upon the apostles as inaugurating the New Covenant foretold by the prophets and thus restoring Israel from her exile. Far from being in discontinuity with the covenantal history of Israel, the New Covenant is a new chapter in that history.

For Luke, the fulfillment of prophecy does not merely serve as a source of apologetic proofs for the teaching of the apostles. Rather, the fact of such fulfillment lies at the heart of his message: What God had promised through the prophets to do for Israel, He has now done through Jesus and the Holy Spirit. Luke sets forth this understanding of the New Covenant in the course of his narrative through his account of the apostles' ministry.

Covenantal History

To grasp the beliefs and intentions of the apostles, one must realize that almost all the leaders of the early Church were Jews. While Gentiles are converted beginning in Acts 10, not a single Gentile leader of the rapidly growing Church is mentioned throughout the whole of Acts. All the leaders of the early Church

were shaped by Israel's covenantal history. God dealt
with mankind's sin by calling Abraham and eventually the twelve tribes of Israel to serve Him as an
elect people through whom all the peoples of the
earth would one day be blessed. Israel then violated
her covenant and fell into sin, for which she was
suffering the curse of Gentile domination (cf. Deut.
28:15; 30:1).[1] However, God promised through the
prophets to send a royal descendant of David—the
Messiah—who would lift the curse and restore Israel
to covenantal relation with God, and thereby allow
Israel finally to fulfill her appointed task of bringing
covenantal blessing to all the peoples of the earth.
The apostles believed that Jesus was this Messiah,
vindicated as such by God through His Resurrection
from the dead.[2] In like manner, God would vindicate
all His people in the end through the resurrection of
the dead, which would occur when Jesus manifested
Himself in glory.

The Abrahamic Promise

The leaders of the early Church considered
themselves the heirs of the Abrahamic covenant.
This belief in the Abrahamic covenant was held as
strongly by the most enthusiastic proponents of the
Gentile mission, such as Paul (cf. Gal. 3:7-8, 14-16, 29;
Rom. 4:13, 16), as by those who were more cautious
toward the Gentiles. Indeed, God's covenantal oath to

---

[1] N. T. Wright, *The New Testament and the People of God*, Christian
Origins and the Question of God, vol. 1 (Minneapolis: Fortress Press,
1992), 268-70.

[2] N. T. Wright, *Jesus and the Victory of God*, Christian Origins and the
Question of God, vol. 2 (Minneapolis: Fortress Press, 1996), 126-27.

Abraham of blessing for all the nations (cf. Gen. 22:16-18) undergirded Paul's conviction that the Gentiles were to be incorporated into the People of God.

However, there was uncertainty—and at times sharp disagreement—about the ongoing status of the Mosaic covenant. Was the New Covenant brought about by Jesus superimposed on the Mosaic covenant, leaving the latter unaltered, or did it bring the Mosaic covenant to its culmination? This was the theological question at the heart of the dispute over whether Gentile converts should be circumcised and required to obey the Mosaic Law (cf. Acts 15:1-2, 5).

The Kingdom of God

In answer to this question, the apostles came to teach that the New Covenant was not an adjunct to the Mosaic covenant, but the miraculous fulfillment of the Abrahamic covenant by the anointed heir of David, as promised in the prophets (cf. Acts 15:14-18). Through the prophet Nathan, God had promised David a descendant whose "kingdom shall be made sure for ever" (2 Sam. 7:16). Yet Israel had fallen into sin and been afflicted with the covenantal curses (cf. Deut. 28:15-68), the most prominent of which was exile. The temporal political power of the Davidic kingdom was destroyed. Thereafter, the great hope of Israel, resounding throughout the prophets, was for the restoration of the kingdom, understood not merely as a temporal political entity, but as God's rule on earth extended from heaven (cf. Is. 52:7). This restoration would be brought about by a new covenant in which God's promise to Abraham of blessing for all the nations would be fulfilled (cf. Jer. 31:31-34).

The apostles believed that Jesus had inaugurated this restored kingdom (cf. Acts 8:12; 14:22; 19:8; 20:25; 28:23). Jesus had proclaimed the good news of the kingdom's arrival, but even more, He had brought it about through His ministry. In His exorcisms and healings, He had shown that the restoration foretold by the prophets had indeed arrived. By demonstrating His power to forgive sins and thus restore Israel to covenantal relation with God, Jesus had shown that He possessed the authority previously reserved to the temple. Jesus is the son of David "greater than Solomon" (Mt. 12:42) who will build a new Temple for His kingdom (cf. Mt. 16:18-19). Jesus is the king, and the kingdom has been inaugurated by His works of power, culminating in His Resurrection and Ascension.

The People of God

Throughout history, covenants were the means God used to choose a people who would receive His revelation and serve Him in accordance with it. The New Covenant was no exception to this pattern. But what was the nature of the people elected by this New Covenant, and what was its relation to the existing nations of the world? The texts of the prophets are quite clear that the New Covenant was to be first and foremost with Israel: "Behold, the days are coming, says the LORD, when I will make a new covenant with the house of Israel and the house of Judah" (Jer. 31:31). Jeremiah's distinct references to the "house of Israel" and the "house of Judah" are significant (cf. Ezek. 34:21-22). The house of Israel refers to the ten tribes of the northern kingdom, which in Jeremiah's day had already been conquered by Assyria and dispersed among the neighboring peoples, while the house of Judah refers to the two tribes of the southern kingdom, which were soon to be conquered by Babylon. The People of God must therefore gather the twelve tribes, most of which were scattered among the Gentiles.

Accordingly, Luke draws attention to the fact that the Church begins with Israelites gathered in "from every nation under heaven" (Acts 2:5). He does not hesitate to use the term "Church" in reference to a period in which the New Covenant community consisted only of Israelites (cf. Acts 5:11; 8:1, 3; 9:31). Peter is similarly emphatic in identifying the New Covenant People of God with the restored Israel (cf. 1 Pet. 2:9-10). Thus, the New Covenant does not create a second People of God alongside Israel, but encompasses all in Israel who would receive the Spirit.

Jew and Gentile United

Yet, during the course of their ministry, the apostles became increasingly aware of God's will to include also the Gentiles within the New Covenant. At the central turning point of Acts, James declares that God has drawn forth from the Gentiles new members of His chosen people (cf. Acts 15:14); no longer to be separated from Israel, the Gentiles have been brought into the "dwelling of David" as foretold by the prophets (Acts 15:16). This new union of Jew and Gentile was produced by the Holy Spirit, who established a spiritual kinship among all members of the People of God (cf. Acts 10:44-47; 15:7-8). Hence, membership in the one People of God did not require submission to the Mosaic Law.

It should not be surprising that the teaching of the apostles met with intense opposition from many Jews, for it ran directly contrary to the theological agenda of the Pharisees, who were a major force within first century Judaism and whose influence extended into the Church (cf. Acts 15:5). The Pharisees sought to reinforce and intensify the Deuteronomic covenant as a bulwark against Gentile influence.[3] They strictly interpreted and extended those precepts of the Mosaic Law that resulted in cultural separation from the Gentiles, believing that only through such separation could the People of God regain its holiness. The apostles' teaching not only undermined the Pharisees' quest for separation, but ultimately contradicted the principle of separation embedded in the Deuteronomic covenant itself.

The New Exodus

A major theme of Luke is that Jesus is the new Moses who leads a new exodus from the bondage of the covenantal curses. Implicitly in his Gospel and explicitly in Acts, Luke describes Jesus as the prophet like Moses foretold by Moses himself (cf. Deut. 18:15-19; Acts 3:22; 7:37). In the Transfiguration, the impending death and Resurrection of Jesus are described as "his departure [*éxodon*], which he was to accomplish at Jerusalem" (Lk. 9:31). Jesus' Resurrection is the "first fruits" of

---

[3] Marcus J. Borg, *Conflict, Holiness, and Politics in the Teachings of Jesus* (Harrisburg: Trinity Press International, 1998), 73-74.

the restored kingdom (1 Cor. 15:20-24), in which the "whole house of Israel" will be brought to life by the Spirit (Ezek. 37:11-14).

Luke continues and extends the new exodus typology in Acts, beginning with Pentecost. Because it occurs fifty days after Passover, Pentecost was associated with God's revelation of the Mosaic Law on Mount Sinai. In first century Judaism, the Sinai theophany was understood as God's greatest act of self-revelation. Philo, for example, describes the Sinai theophany as being marked not only by flames streaming from heaven, but also by articulate speech coming from the flames that all present could understand in a familiar language.[4]

Luke depicts the outpouring of the Holy Spirit at Pentecost as a new revelation parallel to but surpassing that of Sinai, for now the Spirit Himself is given to the People of God as the New Law of the New Covenant, a law inscribed not on tablets of stone but on the hearts of all who receive Him. The decision faced by each Israelite was whether he was willing to repent and receive the Spirit (cf. Acts 2:37-38). Just as the giving of the Mosaic Law was a covenantal test that led to Israel's forty years of wandering in the wilderness, so the giving of the New Law led to the testing of a new "wilderness generation."

The Wilderness Generation

The motif of the wilderness generation condemned to wander for forty years because of Israel's

---

[4] Philo, *Philo in Ten Volumes (and Two Supplementary Volumes)*, trans. F. H. Colson, vol. 7 (Cambridge, Mass.: Harvard University Press, 1937), 23, 29.

repeated apostasy is prominent in the Book of Deuteronomy (cf. Deut. 1:35; 2:7, 14; 32:5, 20) and is perhaps best summarized in Psalm 95:10-11:

> For forty years I loathed that generation and said, "They are a people who err in heart, and they do not regard my ways." Therefore I swore in my anger that they should not enter my rest.

Jesus' frequent references to the wickedness of "this generation" (e.g., Lk. 7:31; 9:41; 11:29-32, 50; 17:25) allude to this Deuteronomic motif and thereby warn of impending judgment for those who reject His call to repentance. These warnings of judgment reach their climax in His prophecy of the destruction of Jerusalem and the Temple within "this generation" (Lk. 21:32).

The apostles carried out their ministry in the shadow of Jesus' prophecy, preaching salvation from "this crooked generation" (Acts 2:40) in a city and Temple they knew to be doomed. They stood at the center of covenantal history, in the calm at the eye of a storm: The sun had darkened, and the veil of the Temple had been rent in two (cf. Lk. 23:45), but still the Temple stood. The lightning had struck, but the thunder had not yet reached the ears of men.

The Last Days

The Book of Acts is set in the tense interval between the two great poles of Jesus' death and Resurrection and the coming destruction of the Temple, a period of which the forty years of the wilderness generation was understood as a type. The New Covenant had been inaugurated, but the Deuteronomic covenant had not yet reached its visible end. Nevertheless, that end could not be far off, for it had been promised within "this generation." The apostles saw themselves as living in the last days of the Deuteronomic covenant, which had shaped Israel's cultural, political, and religious world for over a millennium. Those whose loyalties were centered on the Temple were the chief opponents of Jesus' followers. Hence, Jesus' prophecy of the judgment of Jerusalem undergirded the apostles' hope for the imminent vindication of their faith in Jesus and in the promise of the Gentiles' entry into the kingdom. In the face of persecution, they ceaselessly pursued this hope through the proclamation of the Good News of the kingdom, the baptismal gift of the Spirit, and the Eucharistic celebration of the "powers of the age to come" (Heb. 6:5).

* * *

Questions for Discussion

1. The New Testament describes Jesus as fulfilling the promises made to Abraham.

a. Read Genesis 22:16-18. What is the covenant God makes with Abraham?

_____

_____

_____

b. Read Galatians 3:7-8, 14-16, 29 and Romans 4:13, 16. How does Paul describe the fulfillment of the Abrahamic covenant?

_____

_____

_____

c. In what ways is Abraham a model for our lives as Catholics today?

_____

_____

d. How does the Catholic faith fulfill the promises God made to Abraham?

_____

_____

2. Read Deuteronomy 6:3-5; 10:11-12; 11:11-13; 26:15-16; 28:15 ff.; and 30:1.

a. What are the blessings of the Deuteronomic covenant?

_____

_____

b. What are the curses?

_____

_____

c. How does the Church bring covenantal blessings to all mankind?

_____

_____

3. Read Jeremiah 31:31-34 and Ezekiel 34:22-31. What are the main features of the New Covenant foretold by the prophets?

_____

_____

4. How do the prophets describe the restoration of the kingdom to Israel in the following passages?

a. Isaiah 55:3-5

_____

_____

b. Micah 5:2-4

_____

_____

c. Jeremiah 23:5; 30:8-9; 33:14-15

_____

_____

d. Zechariah 3:8-10; 6:12

_____

_____

e. How does the Church fulfill these passages?

_____

_____

5. Read Hebrews 9:6-9 and 12:18-28. What is the connection between the destruction of the Temple, the end of Mosaic sacrifices, and the institution of the Church?

_____

_____

6. Read Catechism, nos. 781-82, concerning the apostles' teaching that the Church is the People of God.

a. How can this biblical teaching be easily misconstrued by interpreting it in a predominantly secular framework?

_____

_____

b. How does the concept of the People of God deepen our understanding of the Church when its scriptural roots (in both the Old and New Testaments) are taken into account?

_____

_____

7. Read Catechism, nos. 75-76, concerning the apostolic Tradition.

a. How does apostolic Tradition form the basis of our Catholic faith?

_____

_____

b. In what ways are our study and knowledge of both the Old and New Testaments dependent on apostolic Tradition?

_____

_____

CHRIST THE KING
—ACTS 1—

L uke begins Acts with the statement that in his Gospel, he "dealt with all that Jesus began to do and teach" (Acts 1:1), implying that in Acts he will deal with what Jesus continues to do and teach. Accordingly, we find that Acts concerns Jesus' sending of the Holy Spirit to continue His ministry through the apostles. However, before Jesus sends the Holy Spirit, He further prepares the apostles by appearing to them in His risen body for forty days and teaching them about the kingdom of God (cf. Acts 1:3). The period of forty days recalls the similar interval that Moses spent in the cloud of glory upon Mount Sinai:

> Then Moses went up on the mountain, and the cloud covered the mountain. The glory of the LORD settled on Mount Sinai. . . . And Moses entered the cloud, and went up on the mountain. And Moses was on the mountain forty days and forty nights (Ex. 24:15-16, 18).

While on Sinai for those forty days, Moses received detailed instruction from God on the administration of the covenant (cf. Ex. 25-31). For the same period of time, the apostles now receive instruction from Jesus on the reality at the heart of the New Covenant: the kingdom of God.

The Advance of the Kingdom

Jesus chose to spend His last days on earth prior to the Ascension instructing the apostles on the kingdom of God. Indeed, the advance of the kingdom is a central theme of Acts. Luke's second book recounts the beginning of the reign of Christ, first in heaven and then on earth, as Christ extends His rule through the apostles' proclamation of the Gospel. The power to proclaim the Gospel and advance the kingdom does not come from the apostles themselves, but from the Holy Spirit, for whom they must wait (cf. Acts 1:4-5). The Holy Spirit, acting in and through men, brings about the reign of Christ on earth.

Jesus told the apostles that they would receive the Holy Spirit "before many days" had passed (Acts 1:5). Hence, they realized that the outpouring of the Spirit, foretold by the prophets as accompanying the restoration of Israel, was about to commence. The apostles therefore ask Jesus a very natural question: "Lord, will you at this time restore the kingdom to Israel?" (Acts 1:6).

The Twelve Tribes of Israel

The import of the apostles' question turns on the meaning of "Israel." From the time she had entered the promised land, Israel had been constituted by the Deuteronomic covenant.[1] Central to Jesus' ministry, however, was the reconstitution of Israel around Himself and the twelve apostles. Thus, at the Last Supper, He had told the apostles:

> [A]s my Father appointed a kingdom for me, so do I appoint for you that you may eat and drink at my table in my kingdom, and sit on thrones judging the twelve tribes of Israel (Lk. 22:29-30).

---

[1] N. T. Wright, *The New Testament and the People of God*, Christian Origins and the Question of God, vol. 1 (Minneapolis: Fortress Press, 1992), 261.

The "Israel" about whom the apostles now ask is therefore Israel as reconstituted around Jesus and themselves. Their question no more reflects a misunderstanding of the kingdom than does Jesus' own statement above.

From the apostles' perspective, the key phrase in their question is "at this time." They are specifically asking *when* the restoration will be manifested. Jesus answers that they should not seek "to know times or seasons" within the Father's plan (Acts 1:7), but as for the restoration of the kingdom, they will "receive power when the Holy Spirit has come upon" them (Acts 1:8). The power given to them by the Holy Spirit will enable them to proclaim the Gospel as Christ's witnesses and thereby advance the kingdom "in Jerusalem and in all Judea and Samaria and to the end of the earth" (Acts 1:8). This geographic sequence maps out the plot of Luke's narrative, as the apostles spread the Gospel in an ever-widening circle: first to the inhabitants of Jerusalem, then to the Jews in the surrounding province of Judea, then to the mixed remnant of the northern tribes in Samaria, and finally to the nations of the world.

The End of the Earth

Jesus' reference to "the end of the earth" calls to mind the many Old Testament passages that link this phrase with God's fulfillment of His promise to Abraham of a blessing for all the nations. One such passage is found in Isaiah 49 and relates to the restoration of Israel by the servant of the Lord:

It is too light a thing that you should be my servant to raise up the tribes of Jacob and to restore the preserved of Israel; I will give you as a light to the nations, that my salvation may reach *to the end of the earth* (Is. 49:6, emphasis added).

In Isaiah's vision, the blessing of the nations and the restoration of Israel do not merely occur at the same time; rather, the blessing of the nations is the very means by which Israel is restored:

Thus says the Lord GOD: "Behold, I will lift up my hand to the nations, and raise my signal to the peoples; and they shall bring your sons in their bosom, and your daughters shall be carried on their shoulders (Is. 49:22).

Jesus' allusion implies that Isaiah's prophecy will soon be fulfilled through the ministry of the apostles. For those who have ears to hear, Jesus has answered the apostles' question. He who taught them to pray "Thy kingdom come" (Mt. 6:10) has now revealed to them the fulfillment of this prayer.

Coming to the Throne

Any lingering doubts that the apostles may still have had about Jesus were dispelled when "as they were looking on, he was lifted up, and a cloud took him out of their sight" (Acts 1:9). The Ascension was the definitive guarantee of the promise of power that Jesus had given the apostles, for He not only departed from earth, but also entered the divine glory. Jesus was taken up not into the clouds of the sky, but into the cloud of glory that manifests the presence of

God. This was the cloud that descended upon Mount Sinai, accompanied Israel in the wilderness, and filled Solomon's Temple. This was the cloud that overshadowed Jesus during the Transfiguration and from which the Father spoke (cf. Lk. 9:34-35). Thus, Paul describes Jesus as having been "taken up in glory" (1 Tim. 3:16). Within the cloud of glory there is found the throne of God, and from the Ascension onward Jesus is seated on this throne at the right hand of the Father.

The Ascension fulfills Jesus' declaration at His trial that "from now on the Son of man shall be seated at the right hand of the power of God" (Lk. 22:69). Mark reports the additional words, "and coming with the clouds of heaven" (Mk. 14:62), making it clear that Jesus was alluding to the vision of Daniel 7. In this vision, a "son of man" comes "with the clouds of heaven" from earth to the throne of God, signifying heavenly exaltation: "[W]ith the clouds of heaven there came one like a son of man, and he came to the Ancient of Days and was presented before him" (Dan. 7:13). Jesus, the true Son of man, has ascended to the throne in His humanity.

The Victory of the Gospel

The Ascension marks the beginning of Christ's rule over His kingdom and demonstrates His victory over the powers of darkness (cf. Eph. 1:20-21; Col. 2:15). Just before his martyrdom, Stephen

> gazed into heaven and saw the glory of God, and Jesus standing at the right hand of God; and he said, "Behold, I see the heavens opened, and the Son of man standing at the right hand of God" (Acts 7:55-56).

Not only does Christ reign in glory from heaven, but His kingdom continually breaks into the earthly realm, where it is advanced through the witness of His disciples. By the advance of the messianic kingdom throughout the earth, Daniel's vision is progressively fulfilled.

> And to him was given dominion and glory and kingdom, that all peoples, nations, and languages should serve him; his dominion is an everlasting dominion, which shall not pass away, and his kingdom one that shall not be destroyed (Dan. 7:14).

The apostles, therefore, undertake their mission with a sure faith in the forthcoming victory of the Gospel. Although Jesus will no longer be with them physically, they accept His absence without regret, trusting in His promise of the Holy Spirit. This is why they "returned to Jerusalem with great joy" (Lk. 24:52) rather than sadness.

The College of the Twelve

After noting their return to Jerusalem, Luke lists the names of the eleven remaining apostles, emphasizing their ongoing collective identity as a college (cf. Acts 1:13). Peter is listed first, just as he is in the Gospels. At some point during the nine days between the Ascension and Pentecost, "Peter stood up among the brethren" to address them concerning the replacement of Judas (Acts 1:15). To "stand up among the brethren" refers to a formal speech delivered in a synagogue. By describing Peter's speech in this manner, Luke highlights the leadership that Peter exercises immediately following the Ascension. It is Peter who explains the necessity of replacing Judas and sets forth the criterion that candidates must satisfy.

The background for Peter's speech lies in Jesus' teaching that, in the kingdom, the apostles will "sit on thrones judging the twelve tribes of Israel" (Lk. 22:30). Jesus' choice of exactly twelve apostles was not random. Rather, the number symbolizes the apostles' role as covenant representatives around whom the twelve tribes of Israel would be reconstituted. Hence, the apostolic college needed to be restored to its full complement of twelve members for the restoration of Israel to proceed. Ezekiel had prophesied that the restoration of Israel would accompany the outpouring of the Spirit, which Jesus had said was imminent. Therefore, it was urgent that Judas be replaced immediately.

Peter begins his speech by describing the vacancy in the apostolic college created by Judas' betrayal of Jesus (cf. Acts 1:16-19). This vacancy is the result not of Judas's *death* but of his unrepentant *apostasy*, which has disqualified him from being one of the Twelve. Having willfully removed himself from the apostolic college, Judas must now be replaced. In contrast, when James the Elder is martyred by Herod Agrippa in Acts 12:1-2, he is not similarly replaced. Far from having disqualified himself, James has witnessed to his office with his blood.

The Testimony of the Scriptures

Peter then shows that Scripture has provided for the replacement of a disqualified apostle. He first paraphrases Psalm 69:25: "Let his habitation become desolate, and let there be no one to live in it"

(Acts 1:20). The relevance of Peter's reference lies in the fact that Psalm 69 is a "testimony," a passage of the Old Testament that the apostles interpreted as directly pertaining to the life of Jesus.[2] As a result, various portions of this psalm are cited in reference to Jesus at least eleven times in the New Testament. In addition, Psalm 69 is one of the "psalms of the righteous sufferer"[3] in which the speaker is a suffering figure who is persecuted by the wicked for his faithfulness to God. The apostles interpreted these psalms as messianic. Psalm 69 was specifically interpreted as pertaining to Jesus' final ministry in Jerusalem and especially to His Passion. The section from which Peter draws his paraphrase (Ps. 69:21-28) describes the enemies of the sufferer and the curses that befall them. Peter applies this section to Judas, interpreting Psalm 69:25 as describing the terrible end that Judas met after his betrayal (cf. Acts 1:18-19).

Peter's quotation of Psalm 109:8 ("His office let another take") in Acts 1:20 is similar. Like Psalm 69, Psalm 109 is a psalm of the righteous sufferer and was applied by the apostles to Jesus' Passion (cf. Mt. 27:39; Mk. 15:29). The significance of the quotation lies in its reference to an office. Peter evidently considers the role of an apostle to be an office within the kingdom of Israel, one that should be filled in the event of a vacancy.

---

[2] C. H. Dodd, *According to the Scriptures: The Sub-structure of New Testament Theology* (New York: Scribner, 1953), 28-31, 57-60.

[3] Donald Juel, *Messianic Exegesis: Christological Interpretation of the Old Testament in Early Christianity* (Philadelphia: Fortress Press, 1988), 89-131; Joel Marcus, *The Way of the Lord: Christological Exegesis of the Old Testament in the Gospel of Mark* (Louisville: Westminster/John Knox Press, 1992), 176-79, 190.

Why did Peter and the apostles consider the psalms of the righteous sufferer to be directly applicable to the life of Jesus? From the distribution in the New Testament of references to these Old Testament passages, it can be shown that their interpretation as messianic predates the composition of even the earliest portions of the New Testament. For his part, Luke leaves no doubt that the framework of the apostles' exegesis came from Jesus Himself, for He taught them how to find "everything written about [him] in the law of Moses and the prophets and the psalms" (Lk. 24:44).

Officers of the New Temple

Peter concludes his speech by stating the fundamental requirement that any candidate to replace Judas must meet: He must have been a disciple "during all the time that the Lord Jesus went in and out among us, beginning from the baptism of John until the day when he was taken up from us" (Acts 1:21-22). Such a candidate would not only have heard Jesus' teaching at first hand during His ministry, but would also have witnessed Jesus' post-Resurrection appearances, enabling him to "become with us a witness to his resurrection" (Acts 1:22). This requirement establishes an essential distinction between the apostles and the bishops (overseers) who will be appointed later in Acts (cf. Acts 20:28). The apostles are eyewitnesses to Jesus' life, death, and Resurrection, whereas the bishops, in general, are not.

The apostles then nominate two men, Joseph and Matthias, who meet the above requirement.

However, rather than choosing between the two candidates on their own authority, the apostles ask God to "show which one of these two thou hast chosen to take the place in this ministry and apostleship from which Judas turned aside" (Acts 1:24-25). The method used by the apostles to ascertain God's will in the selection was to cast lots. The casting of lots was a traditional Israelite means for determining God's will and, from the time of David down to the first century A.D., was used to select Aaronites for divine worship. First Chronicles 24 describes how David organized into divisions of roughly equal size the families descended from Aaron. On a periodic basis, lots would be cast to choose which division would perform their offices of ministry (cf. 1 Chron. 24:3, 19). The descendants of Aaron thus chosen to serve in the Temple are described as "officers of the sanctuary and officers of God" (1 Chron. 24:5). Likewise, the apostles see their role as that of officers serving in the new temple of God, the Mystical Body of Christ.

*   *   *

Questions for Discussion

1. Read Acts 1:4-5 and Catechism, nos. 1266, 1831. How do we use the gifts of the Holy Spirit in our own lives?

_____

_____

_____

2. Read Acts 1:8, Daniel 7:14, and Catechism, no. 664.

a. How is Jesus' Ascension and the spread of the Church a fulfillment of Daniel's prophecy?

_____

_____

b. How should the reign of Christ from heaven and the unfolding victory of the Gospel govern our attitude and approach toward evangelization?

_____

_____

c. How is the kingship of Christ manifested today? What can we do to further His kingdom?

_____

_____

_____

3. Read Luke 22:29-30, in which Christ describes the role of the apostles.

a. Why must there be twelve apostles?

_____

_____

b. How is the Eucharist at the center of the kingdom of God?

_____

_____

4. Read Matthew 6:10.

a. Is the kingdom entirely the work of God, or must we work in conjunction with the Holy Spirit for its advance?

_____

b. How does the apostolate relate to the life of prayer?

_____

_____

5. Read Psalm 69. How does the psalm describe the end of Christ's life?

_____

_____

6. Other psalms that foretell the Passion of Jesus included Psalms 22, 27, 28, 89, and 109. In what ways do they do so?

_____

_____

THE CHURCH OF THE LAST DAYS
—ACTS 2:1-21—

Luke depicts the outpouring of the Holy Spirit on Pentecost (Acts 2) as marking both a beginning and an end. At last, the Holy Spirit is given to the People of God as a New Law for a New Covenant. Accompanying the gift of the Spirit, however, is the sign of prophecy in other languages, a sign of impending judgment on the Mosaic covenant.

The Giving of the Law

In the Old Testament, Pentecost was known as the Feast of Weeks and originally had an agricultural significance. It came to be called *Pentecost* (from the Greek word for fiftieth) by Greek-speaking Jews because it was celebrated fifty days after Passover. Shortly after the original Passover, the Jews arrived at Mount Sinai and received the Mosaic Law (cf. Ex. 19:1-6). Because Pentecost came shortly after Passover, the Jews came to associate it with the giving of the Law. In the great theophany that accompanied the giving of the Mosaic Law, God descended in the form of fire and with the sound of a trumpet:

> On the morning of the third day there were thunders and lightnings, and a thick cloud upon the mountain, and a very loud trumpet blast. . . . And Mount Sinai was wrapped in smoke, because the LORD descended upon it in fire. . . . And as the sound of the trumpet grew louder and louder, Moses spoke, and God answered him in thunder (Ex. 19:16, 18-19).

Since God is said to have answered Moses, there is an implication that the sound contained intelligible speech. Philo of Alexandria, a first century Jewish theologian, makes the element of intelligible speech explicit in his description of the theophany. He states that God manifested Himself in a great sound:

> [G]iving shape and tension to the air and changing it to a flaming fire, [there] sounded forth like the breath through a trumpet an articulate voice so loud that it appeared to be equally audible to the farthest as well as the nearest. . . . Then from the midst of the fire that streamed from heaven there sounded forth to their utter amazement a voice, for the flame became articulate speech in a language familiar to the audience.[1]

The giving of the Law on Mount Sinai was thus characterized by three signs: a great sound, streams of fire, and miraculous, intelligible speech. The same three signs are manifested when the apostles gather together on the first Pentecost after the Resurrection.

> And suddenly a sound came from heaven like the rush of a mighty wind, and it filled all the house where they were sitting. And there appeared to them tongues as of fire, distributed and resting on each one of them. And they were all filled with the Holy Spirit and began to speak in other tongues, as the Spirit gave them utterance (Acts 2:2-4).

---

[1] Philo, *On the Decalogue* 9:33; 11:46 in *Philo in Ten Volumes (and Two Supplementary Volumes)*, trans. F. H. Colson, vol. 7 (Cambridge, Mass.: Harvard University Press, 1937), 23, 29.

The New Law of the Spirit

The gift of the Holy Spirit at Pentecost is thus a new theophany parallel to the giving of the Mosaic Law on Sinai. The prophetic background of the gift of the Spirit shows that the notion of law-giving is central to the parallelism. In Ezekiel, God promised that He would one day place His Spirit within His people, giving them a new heart with which to observe His Law.

> A new heart I will give you, and a new spirit I will put within you; and I will take out of your flesh the heart of stone and give you a heart of flesh. And I will put my spirit within you, and cause you to walk in my statutes and be careful to observe my ordinances (Ezek. 36:26-27; cf. 37:14).

In Jeremiah, God promised that the Law would be written on the hearts of His people, thereby constituting a "new covenant" (cf. Jer. 31:31, 33). Ezekiel's indwelling Spirit and Jeremiah's interior law are closely linked, for it is the Spirit who brings about the fulfillment of the God's Law. Lacking the Spirit, Israel had repeatedly shown herself unable to keep the Mosaic Law, from the apostasy of the golden calf (cf. Ex. 32) to the Babylonian exile. In contrast, with the New Covenant, the Spirit is poured out on the People of God. As a result, the New Covenant will "not [be] like the covenant which I made with their fathers when I took them by the hand to bring them out of the land of Egypt, my covenant which they broke" (Jer. 31:32). Pentecost fulfills the prophecies of Ezekiel and Jeremiah and is, therefore, not merely a repetition of the Sinai theophany but greatly surpasses it, for the Spirit now indwells the People of God as the New Law of the New Covenant (cf. Rom. 8:1-2).

Israel Reunited

The crowd that heard the apostles consisted of Jews "from every nation under heaven" (Acts 2:5) on pilgrimage to Jerusalem for Pentecost. By the first century A.D., Jews were living throughout the Gentile nations of the Mediterranean and Near East. The ten tribes of the northern kingdom of Israel had been dispersed among the surrounding nations by the Assyrians, while the two tribes of the southern kingdom of Judah had been exiled by the Babylonians. Nevertheless, God was to make the New Covenant with a reunited Israel drawn from the twelve tribes, "with the house of Israel and the house of Judah" (Jer. 31:31). Thus, the Holy Spirit inaugurates the Church with Israelites gathered in from the dispersion, representing all of Israel.[2] This ingathering of the exiles is the fulfillment of the prophecy of Isaiah 11.

> In that day the Lord will extend his hand yet a second time to recover the remnant which is left of his people, from Assyria, from Egypt, from Pathros, from Ethiopia, from Elam, from Shinar, from Hamath, and from the coastlands of the sea. He will . . . assemble the outcasts of Israel, and gather the dispersed of Judah from the four corners of the earth (Is. 11:11-12).

---

[2] J. Bradley Chance, *Jerusalem, the Temple, and the New Age in Luke-Acts* (Macon, Ga.: Mercer University Press, 1988), 73.

Isaiah 11 is a prophecy of the Messiah and His work of restoration. The prophecy begins with a description of the Spirit resting on the Messiah and bestowing His gifts:

> There shall come forth a shoot from the stump of Jesse, and a branch shall grow out of his roots. And the Spirit of the LORD shall rest upon him, the spirit of wisdom and understanding, the spirit of counsel and might, the spirit of knowledge and the fear of the LORD (Is. 11:1-2).

With the outpouring of the Spirit at Pentecost, all who repent and are baptized (cf. Acts 2:38) receive the same gifts of the Spirit.

Foreign Tongues

Upon being "filled with the Holy Spirit," the disciples "began to speak in other tongues" (Acts 2:4). The word "tongue" in this context simply means "language," so that to speak in "other tongues" is to speak in languages other than one's own. The miracle worked by the Holy Spirit is that the apostles are able to speak in languages known to their audience but not to themselves (cf. Acts 2:6, 8). Although the apostles speak in Aramaic, their speech on this occasion is heard and understood in the foreign languages of their audience rather than in Aramaic. The crowd hears the apostles speak of "the mighty works of God" (Acts 2:11) in the manner of the prophets, proclaiming to Israel the ways in which God has fulfilled His covenantal promises.

The miracle of speech in foreign languages has a prophetic background in Isaiah 28, where it is

intended for unbelieving Jews as a sign of the impending destruction of Jerusalem (cf. 1 Cor. 14:21).[3] As with
Old Testament prophecy generally, the sign of foreign
languages has the function of proclaiming a covenant
judgment. Isaiah 28 concerns God's judgment of
Jerusalem through conquest by a foreign army.
Because the rulers of Jerusalem had rejected Isaiah's
prophecy given plainly in Hebrew, they would instead
be addressed in a foreign language.

> [B]y men of strange lips and with an alien tongue
> the LORD will speak to this people . . . that they may
> go, and fall backward, and be broken, and snared,
> and taken. Therefore hear the word of the LORD,
> you scoffers, who rule this people in Jerusalem!
> (Is. 28:11, 13-14)

This foreign speech would be a sign of impending
judgment, "a decree of destruction from the Lord GOD
of hosts upon the whole land" (Is. 28:22).

Witness in Jerusalem

Just as Peter earlier addressed the company of
believers about the replacement of Judas, so he
addresses the crowd in Jerusalem to explain the
remarkable event now taking place. Luke highlights
the fact that Peter exercises his leadership not only
within the nascent Church but in the public forum as
well. Peter's speech in Acts 2 is the first example of
the apostles' preaching and becomes a model for the
apostolic speeches that follow.

---

[3] Craig A. Evans and James A. Sanders, *Luke and Scripture: The Function
of Sacred Tradition in Luke-Acts* (Minneapolis: Fortress Press, 1993), 215.

Peter directs his remarks to the "[m]en of Judea and all who dwell in Jerusalem" (Acts 2:14), which is striking in that Luke has already reported that many in the crowd were not residents of Judea or Jerusalem, but pilgrims from distant lands. Peter focuses his remarks on Jerusalem to prepare for the passage from Joel that he is about to quote (Joel 2:28-32), which concerns above all those "in Mount Zion and in Jerusalem" (Joel 2:32). This passage from Joel develops Ezekiel's theme of the outpouring of the Spirit.

Peter uses the passage to explain the Spirit's inauguration of the kingdom of God. Luke has shown in Acts 1 that prior to His Ascension, Jesus instructed the apostles for forty days about the kingdom (cf. Acts 1:3) and told them to wait in Jerusalem for the Holy Spirit (cf. Acts 1:4-5). Having received this instruction, the apostles are able to identify without hesitation the event now unfolding with the outpouring of the Spirit described by Ezekiel and Joel. Luke has carefully included in his narrative everything needed to show that the outpouring of the Spirit at Pentecost inaugurates the restored kingdom, Israel reconstituted within the New Covenant. The Holy Spirit guides the apostles to rule this reconstituted Israel and carry on the work of Christ.

The Last Days

Peter begins his speech to the crowd by declaring that the event now taking place

is what was spoken by the prophet Joel: "And in the last days it shall be, God declares, that I will pour out my Spirit upon all flesh, and your sons and your daughters shall prophesy" (Acts 2:16-17; cf. Joel 2:28).

The "last days," Peter plainly indicates, have arrived.
The theme of the "last days" appears frequently in
the prophets, where it is associated with the restoration of Israel (e.g., Hos. 3:5; Is. 2:2). This restoration,
however, can come only with the "new covenant . . .
not like the [Mosaic] covenant which I made with their
fathers when I took them . . . out of the land of Egypt"
(Jer. 31:31-32). Hence, the "last days" are precisely
the last days of the Mosaic covenant, which, in its
Deuteronomic form, had governed the cultural,
political, and religious life of the People of God for
over a millennium. Peter explains in his first epistle
that the last days have arrived with the manifestation
of the Incarnate Son: "He was destined before the
foundation of the world but was made manifest at the
end of the times for your sake" (1 Pet. 1:20, emphasis
added). The same understanding of the last days is
also found elsewhere in the New Testament:

> In many and various ways God spoke of old to our
> fathers by the prophets; but in these *last days* he has
> spoken to us by a Son. . . . [H]e has appeared once
> for all at the *end of the age* to put away sin by the sac-
> rifice of himself (Heb. 1:1-2; 9:26, emphasis added).

The last days, therefore, begin with the inauguration of the New Covenant and continue until the
Deuteronomic covenant visibly ends with the
destruction of the Temple. Thus, the last days are a
transitional period of overlap between the
Deuteronomic and New Covenants. In his later
speech at the Temple, Peter declares that "all the
prophets who have spoken, from Samuel and those
who came afterwards, also proclaimed these days"

(Acts 3:24). The transitional period of the last days will continue until "the day of the Lord comes, the great and manifest day" (Acts 2:20; cf. Joel 2:31), when Jerusalem would be judged and the Temple destroyed. This day of judgment could not be far off, for Jesus had promised it within "this generation" (Lk. 21:32). The apostles looked forward to this day as one of deliverance from persecution for the faithful "who by God's power are guarded through faith for a salvation ready to be revealed in the last time" (1 Pet. 1:5).

The Gift of the Spirit

The first part of the passage Saint Peter quotes from Joel describes the outpouring of the Spirit as bestowing the charism of prophecy:

> [Y]our sons and your daughters shall prophesy, and your young men shall see visions, and your old men shall dream dreams; yea, and on my menservants and my maidservants in those days I will pour out my Spirit; and they shall prophesy (Acts 2:17-18).

The background for this passage is found in Numbers 11, in which Moses required assistance to "bear the burden of the people" (Num. 11:17). Because of this burden, God instructed Moses to select seventy elders of Israel to assist him. The Holy Spirit and the charism of prophesy would no longer be given to Moses alone but also to these elders. Following God's instructions, Moses

> gathered seventy men of the elders of the people, and placed them round about the tent. Then the LORD came down in the cloud and spoke to him, and

> took some of the spirit that was upon him and put it
> upon the seventy elders; and when the spirit rested
> upon them, they prophesied (Num. 11:24-25).

Two of the appointed elders were left in the camp,
where they received the Spirit and began to prophesy
on their own. When Joshua heard of this apparent
irregularity, he asked Moses to stop the two. Moses,
however, replied, "Would that all the LORD's people
were prophets, that the LORD would put his spirit
upon them!" (Num. 11:29)

Joel 2 prophesies the fulfillment of Moses' desire.
The fact that the Spirit is poured out on "all flesh"
(2:28) indicates that He no longer restricts Himself to
a limited number of elders, but is available to all
within the New Covenant. Yet, this availability of the
Spirit implies a covenant judgment for each person.
Reception of the Spirit is not unconditional, but
rather requires an active response on the part of the
one who would receive Him:

> Repent, and be baptized every one of you in the
> name of Jesus Christ for the forgiveness of your sins;
> and you shall receive the gift of the Holy Spirit. . . .
> Save yourselves from this crooked generation
> (Acts 2:38, 40).

Apocalyptic Signs

Just as Pentecost marked the giving of the Mosaic
Law prior to the forty-year wandering of the wilderness generation, so the giving of the New Law of the
Spirit initiates a similar period of trial for "this crooked
generation" (Acts 2:40) of Israelites. This period of trial
would culminate in the judgment of Jerusalem, which
Joel describes in apocalyptic language:

> And I will show wonders in the heaven above
> and signs on the earth beneath, blood, and fire,
> and vapor of smoke; the sun shall be turned into
> darkness and the moon into blood, before the
> day of the Lord comes, the great and manifest day
> (Acts 2:19-20; cf. Joel 2:30-31).

Apocalyptic literature is a prophetic genre that employs a system of metaphors to reveal the theological significance of historical events. A set of metaphors commonly used in apocalyptic literature involves celestial bodies, with a celestial disaster indicating the destruction of a city or nation (e.g., Is. 13:9-10; 34:4-5; Ezek. 32:7-8). The apocalyptic language in Joel 2 closely parallels Jesus' description of the destruction of Jerusalem.

> Jerusalem will be trodden down by the Gentiles,
> until the times of the Gentiles are fulfilled. And
> there will be signs in sun and moon and stars, and
> upon the earth distress of nations (Lk. 21:24-25).

The similarity between these two passages is not a coincidence. In His discourse, Jesus drew on the prophetic tradition of which Joel 2 is a part, just as Peter now does in his Pentecost speech.

Escape from Jerusalem

Peter completes his quotation with the first part of Joel 2:32: "And it shall be that whoever calls on the name of the Lord shall be saved" (Acts 2:21). Here again the element of covenant judgment is emphasized; the New Covenant will not save all unconditionally, but only those who "call on the

name of the Lord." It might seem that the salvation
in question in Acts 2:21 is exclusively eternal, but the
remainder of Joel 2:32 suggests that this salvation
also has a temporal dimension: "[F]or in Mount Zion
and in Jerusalem there shall be those who escape, as
the LORD has said, and among the survivors shall be
those whom the LORD calls" (Joel 2:32). The fact that
"in Jerusalem there shall be those who escape"
implies that many would not escape, and, in fact,
many did not. Josephus, a first century Jewish historian, relates that 1.1 million Jews were killed in the
Roman siege and capture of Jerusalem in A.D. 70,
while Eusebius, a fourth century Church historian,
reports that the Christians of Jerusalem left the city
before the siege began.

* * *

Questions for Discussion
1. Read Ezekiel 36:26-27 and Joel 2:28, which foretell
the outpouring of the Holy Spirit on the restored
Israel. How is the outpouring manifested in Acts 2?

_____

_____

_____

2. Read Isaiah 11:1-2 and Catechism, nos. 1303,
1830-31.

a. What are the seven gifts of the Holy Spirit?

_____

_____

b. How do these gifts relate to the spiritual works of mercy?

_____

_____

c. How are these gifts central to any true apostolate?

_____

_____

3. Read Romans 8:5-17, where Saint Paul describes Christian life as following the "law of the Spirit" (Rom. 8:2). How do the sacraments enable us to follow the law of the Spirit?

_____

_____

4. Read Acts 2:14, where Peter exercises his leadership among the apostles by addressing the pilgrims in Jerusalem. Do we hear and recognize the preaching of Peter in the teaching of his successor, the pope?

_____

5. Read Acts 2:17 and 3:24, which refer to the last days. Does Peter consider the last days to be present at the time of his ministry?

_____

THE PREACHING OF PETER
—ACTS 2:22-47—

I n Acts 2:22-36, Peter proclaims the recent events
of Jesus' death, descent into Hades, Resurrection,
and exaltation, using quotations from Psalms
16 and 110 to show that Jesus is the risen Messiah
of Israel. When Paul gives his first great speech as
a Christian missionary at Antioch of Pisidia
(cf. Acts 13:16-41), he employs the Psalms in a
very similar manner.

Peter speaks "directly of the responsibility of those
who had consigned Jesus to death,"[1] the "[m]en of
Israel" now gathered before him, who had deliber-
ately "crucified and killed" Jesus "by the hands of
lawless men," the pagan Romans (Acts 2:22-23). He
indicts these men not as Jews—he himself and all the
disciples are Jews—but for the evil they committed
in rejecting the Messiah and aiding the Jewish
authorities to put Him to death. Yet, Peter tells them,
though Jesus was condemned by the Sanhedrin and
by Pilate, He has been vindicated by God and raised
from the dead (cf. Acts 2:24).

David's Prophecy

To explain Jesus' Resurrection, Peter quotes Psalm
16:8-11 and applies it to Jesus' descent into Hades,
Resurrection, and exaltation. Peter's choice of a psalm
as the basis of his exposition may seem unusual, but
the Psalms were among the most important writings
of the Old Testament for the apostles' presentation of

---

[1] Pope John Paul II, General Audience (November 8, 1989), no. 4.

Jesus as Messiah.[2] Using a common rhetorical technique, Peter refrains from quoting the last line of the psalm, knowing that it will echo in the minds of his audience: "[I]n thy right hand are pleasures for evermore" (Ps. 16:11).

In Psalm 16, David expresses his confidence in God's providential care and protection, trusting that God will "not abandon [his] soul to Hades" (Acts 2:27). Peter, however, observes that the psalm cannot exclusively refer to David himself, for David has died and been buried (cf. Acts 2:29) and, unlike Jesus, has not yet been raised from the dead. Thus, the psalm must have a messianic meaning.

Peter is not merely asserting that David is a type of the Messiah—although that also is true. Rather, Peter is teaching that David wrote with a kind of contemplative vision that the Church Fathers would later call *theoria*. As a prophet (cf. Acts 2:30), David saw in the present realities of his own life the future realities of the Messiah, in whom the psalm would be perfectly fulfilled in its literal sense (cf. Acts 2:31).[3] The basis for David's prophetic foresight was the covenant oath that God had sworn to him (cf. Acts 2:30; Ps. 89:3-4), promising that He would raise up a descendant of his as king, and that the throne of this king would last forever (cf. 2 Sam. 7:12-13). The angel Gabriel declared at the Annunciation that Jesus would fulfill this promise (cf. Lk. 1:32-33).

---

[2] Martin Hengel, *Studies in Early Christology* (Edinburgh: T&T Clark, 1995), 220.

[3] Bertrand de Margerie, S.J., *An Introduction to the History of Exegesis: The Greek Fathers*, vol. 1 (Petersham, Mass.: Saint Bede's Publications, 1993), 176-78.

The Right Hand of God

Peter then alludes to the unquoted last line of Psalm 16 to show that Jesus, having been raised from the dead (cf. Acts 2:32), has also been "exalted at the right hand of God" and given "the promise of the Holy Spirit" (Acts 2:33). The "pleasures" (Ps. 16:11) that Jesus receives at the Father's right hand consist in His exaltation by the Father in the unity of the Holy Spirit. Peter's reference to an unquoted part of Psalm 16 illustrates an important principle: The Old Testament text that a New Testament author has in mind is usually not limited to the portion he explicitly quotes, but also includes the surrounding context.

"[H]aving received from the Father the promise of the Holy Spirit," Jesus has now "poured out" the Spirit upon His disciples, resulting in the prophetic speech in many languages that initially drew the crowd's attention (Acts 2:33). At the Ascension, Jesus was exalted by the Father to exercise lordship over creation on the Father's behalf. At Pentecost, Jesus in turn pours out the Holy Spirit to exercise lordship within the Church on Jesus' behalf. The Father reigns through the Son, and the Son reigns in the Spirit.

Exaltation of the Messiah

Peter elaborates on his explanation of Psalm 16:11 with a citation of Psalm 110:1. The latter is one of the most frequently cited Old Testament verses in the New Testament and serves as a key testimony for the preaching of Jesus as Messiah. Peter interprets the verse in terms of the exaltation of the Messiah and the subjection of His enemies. Peter again draws out the contrast between David and the Messiah, "[f]or

David did not ascend into the heavens," but the Messiah has done so and is seated at the right hand of God (Acts 2:34). Hence, the throne of David's descendant (cf. 2 Sam. 7:13) is the heavenly throne on which the Messiah is now seated.

While the Messiah now reigns, He does so in the context of "enemies" (Acts 2:35) who are only gradually subdued. Peter understands these enemies primarily as the evil powers of the angelic realm (cf. 1 Pet. 3:22), though their earthly manifestation is all too human. The Messiah's reign will continue until God has subjected all of these enemies and made them His footstool. The second half of Psalm 110:1 points to an expanse of time between the exaltation and the final judgment. God has appointed a period for the offer of salvation to go out through the Church, subduing unbelief through repentance and obedience to Christ.

The Ascension marks the inauguration of Christ's reign, which is why it was essential that the apostles witness it. Having seen the Ascension with their own eyes, the apostles can confidently testify to Israel that the son of David now sits on His throne. Jesus is the exalted king, living and reigning with the Father, and has given the Holy Spirit to the Church as an efficacious sign of His power and glory.

In Acts 2:36, Peter reaches the central conclusion of the speech, declaring to "all the house of Israel" that God has made Jesus "both Lord and Christ." Since Jesus has been exalted to the right hand of God, He is the one whom David addresses as "Lord." He now exercises the Father's lordship over creation and is thus the "Lord" in whose name one must be saved (Acts 2:21; cf. Joel 2:32). Hence, Peter's preaching of the kingdom of God centers on Jesus' messianic kingship. Since Jesus' enthronement has fulfilled the oath that God swore to David, He is "Christ," the Messiah of Israel. The disciples of Jesus are members of the restored Davidic kingdom over which Jesus the Messiah now reigns.

Repentance and Baptism

In response to Peter's words, the men are "cut to the heart" (Acts 2:37), recognizing their guilt in supporting the murder of the Messiah. Their recognition of guilt is itself a work of the Holy Spirit, who convicts the world of sin, which stems from unbelief (cf. Jn. 16:7-9). The men ask, "Brethren, what shall we do?" (Acts 2:37), and Peter replies, "Repent, and be baptized" (Acts 2:38).

Repentance (*metánoia*) is a complete change of heart and mind involving a judgment upon the past and a new direction for the future. It is one of the necessary dispositions for initial justification, following faith and hope and preceding the charity bestowed with Baptism. Peter exhorts the people to be baptized "for the forgiveness (*áphesin*) of [their] sins" (Acts 2:38), for which repentance alone is not sufficient. The word Peter uses for forgiveness literally means release, as in the release of captives. Jesus came to release those in captivity because of sin (cf. Lk. 4:18; Is. 61:1), and the apostles now carry out His messianic ministry. Peter declares that the Baptism of the New Covenant bestows "the gift of the Holy Spirit" (Acts 2:38). This Baptism is administered by the apostles as commanded by Christ for the advance of His kingdom.

The Promise

The gift of the Holy Spirit bestowed in Baptism fulfills the promise given to Abraham and through him to all of Israel, "to you and to your children" (Acts 2:39). In His call to Abram, God promised that His blessing would extend through Abram to all the nations of the earth: "I will bless those who bless you, and him who curses you I will curse; and by you all the families of the earth shall bless themselves" (Gen. 12:3). After Abraham demonstrated his faith by his willingness to sacrifice Isaac, God confirmed the promise of universal blessing with a covenant oath:

> By myself I have sworn, says the LORD, because you have done this, and have not withheld your son, your only son, I will indeed bless you, and . . . by your descendants shall all the nations of the earth bless themselves (Gen. 22:16-18).

Paul explains that the promised blessing is received through Baptism because this sacrament of faith incorporates one into the Body of Christ:

> For as many of you as were baptized into Christ have put on Christ. . . . And if you are Christ's, then you are Abraham's offspring, heirs according to promise (Gal. 3:27, 29).

If the promised blessing is to be received by all the nations, then Baptism cannot be limited to Israel but must be made available to all, even "to all that are far off" (Acts 2:39). The phrase "far off" refers not to geographic but to spiritual distance and was used to designate the Gentiles (cf. Eph. 2:13, 17). Hence,

Peter's understanding of the promised blessing anticipates the mission to the Gentiles, a mission that encompasses "every one whom the Lord our God calls" (Acts 2:39).

This Crooked Generation

Luke indicates that he has not included the whole of Peter's speech but has summarized the final portion, in which Peter exhorted the men "with many other words" to save themselves from "this crooked generation" (Acts 2:40). As with Jesus' references to the wickedness of "this generation" (Lk. 21:32 et al.), Peter is alluding to Israel's wilderness generation as a type or pattern of the present generation. The first Passover immediately preceded the crossing of the Red Sea and was soon followed by the giving of the Law; the Last Supper immediately preceded the death and Resurrection of Jesus and was soon followed by the giving of the Spirit. The Israelites wandered for forty years in the wilderness because of their unfaithful refusal to enter the promised land (cf. Num. 14:20-35), with the result that those who had refused to enter died before crossing the Jordan; Israel restored by Christ would hold out the offer of salvation for forty years in Jerusalem in the face of intense persecution, until those who refused to accept the Gospel were destroyed along with the city and Temple.

Many, however, did accept the Gospel, beginning with "about three thousand souls" on Pentecost alone (Acts 2:41). The power of the Holy Spirit does triumph over unbelief in those "whom the Lord our God calls" to Himself (Acts 2:39), extending the reign of Christ and adding believers to His Church. The apostles' mission to Jerusalem operated under the keen awareness that it is Christ, enthroned in heaven, who directs the Church's evangelization.

The Church of Jerusalem

After relating the events of Pentecost from which the Church of Jerusalem emerged, Luke then describes the chief characteristics of that Church. The believers "devoted themselves to the apostles' teaching" (Acts 2:42), which centered on the oral transmission of the memorized words and deeds of Jesus and the messianic interpretation and application of the Old Testament. This teaching would form the Tradition handed down within the Church. Likewise, the believers devoted themselves to "fellowship, to the breaking of bread and the prayers" (Acts 2:42).

These three elements of the Church's life are inseparably linked with one another. Fellowship (*koinōnía*) is a participation in the Mystical Body of Christ through the sacramental Body of Christ:

> The cup of blessing which we bless, is it not a participation (*koinōnía*) in the blood of Christ? The bread which we break, is it not a participation in the body of Christ? Because there is one bread, we who are many are one body, for we all partake of the one bread (1 Cor. 10:16-17).

Fellowship or communion is thus brought about in the Church through the reality of Christ's Eucharistic presence in the power of the Holy Spirit. The

Eucharist, or "breaking of the bread," is not a mere memorial service, but a real participation in the Body of the risen Messiah. In the Eucharist, the Church sits at table with the King, fulfilling His promise "that you may eat and drink at my table in my kingdom" (Lk. 22:30).

"And fear came upon every soul; and many wonders and signs were done through the apostles" (Acts 2:43). As the glory of the Lord had filled the tabernacle in the wilderness and the Temple in Jerusalem, so it now fills the new temple, the Body of Christ. This glory is manifested in the apostles' ministry, which advances the reign of the Messiah and continues His mighty works.

* * *

Questions for Discussion

1. Read Peter's sermon in Acts 2:14-36. Note the connection between the Ascension, in which Christ is enthroned and exalted, and Pentecost, in which He sends us the Holy Spirit.

a. What does the reign of Jesus Christ from heaven mean for us here and now?

_____

_____

b. How ought the kingship of Christ to affect

our families?

_____

_____

our workplaces?

_____

_____

our colleges and universities?

_____

_____

our government?

_____

_____

2. Read Psalms 16 and 110, keeping in mind Peter's use of these psalms in his Pentecost sermon.

a. What insights have you gained into Peter's sermon?

_____

_____

b. How would these insights have been more evident to listeners in Peter's day?

_____

_____

c. How does Peter's use of these psalms show that David is a type of Jesus?

_____

_____

3. Read Catechism, no. 129, which discusses how, as an ancient adage puts it, "the New Testament lies hidden in the Old, and the Old Testament is unveiled in the New."

a. List some of the ways in which Peter applies this principle in his Pentecost sermon.

_____

_____

b. How can we apply this principle in our study of Scripture?

_____

_____

4. Read Catechism, nos. 948 and 950, concerning communion in the Body of Christ.

a. How is Eucharistic Communion the basis of the Communion of the Saints?

_____

_____

b. How has our participation in the Eucharistic Body of Christ led us to strengthen and build the Mystical Body of Christ through our apostolate?

_____

_____

c. In what way does the power of the Holy Spirit make this work possible?

_____

_____

5

The Ministry of Peter
—Acts 3-5—

Following Pentecost, Peter immediately sets about exercising his leadership within the restored Israel through his preaching and works of power. He heals a lame man (cf. Acts 3:1-10), preaches in the Temple (cf. Acts 3:11-26), answers the Jerusalem establishment on behalf of John and himself (cf. Acts 4:5-12), cures the sick (cf. Acts 5:12-16), and speaks for the Twelve before the Sanhedrin (cf. Acts 5:27-32).

The Lame Shall Leap

In Jerusalem, the apostles continue to worship in the Temple regularly (cf. Acts 2:46). As Peter and John are going up to the Temple, they encounter a man "lame from birth" (Acts 3:2) who came to the Temple to beg for alms. Peter heals the lame man "in the name of Jesus Christ of Nazareth" and restores his ability to walk (Acts 3:6). The man's response is immediate and dramatic: "[L]eaping up he stood and walked and entered the temple with them, walking and leaping and praising God" (Acts 3:8). Luke's description of the lame man's "leaping" and "praising God" recalls Isaiah's depiction of the restoration of Israel:

> [T]hen shall the lame man leap like a hart, and . . . the ransomed of the LORD shall return, and come to Zion with singing; everlasting joy shall be upon their heads; they shall obtain joy and gladness, and sorrow and sighing shall flee away (Is. 35:6, 10).

Jesus described His own healings in terms of this
passage from Isaiah (cf. Mt. 11:5). Like Jesus' healings, Peter's healing of the lame man is intended to
show that the restoration of Israel foretold by
Isaiah is now underway.

When the sight of the lame man now healed
draws a crowd, Peter seizes the opportunity to
address those gathered. As in his Pentecost sermon,
he addresses them as "men of Israel" (Acts 2:22;
3:12), for he will appeal to them as the heirs of
Abraham, Isaac, and Jacob. "[T]he God of Abraham
and of Isaac and of Jacob, the God of our fathers" has
vindicated Jesus, for He has "glorified his servant
Jesus, whom you delivered up [*paredōkate*] and
denied in the presence of Pilate, when he had
decided to release him" (Acts 3:13). Peter's description
of Jesus closely follows that of Isaiah's suffering
servant: "Behold, my servant shall prosper, he shall be
exalted and lifted up" (Is. 52:13), but first His soul
will be "delivered up" (*paredóthē*) to death (Is. 53:12,
Septuagint).[1] Peter indicts the witnesses of the healing
for their complicity in the death of Jesus, sharply
contrasting the "Holy and Righteous One" (Acts 3:14)
with the wickedness of His rejection. Indeed, the
one whom they killed was the "Author of life," but
God reversed their verdict and raised Him from the
dead (Acts 3:15).

---

[1] Joel Marcus, *The Way of the Lord: Christological Exegesis of the Old
Testament in the Gospel of Mark* (Louisville: Westminster/John Knox
Press, 1992), 193-94.

All That God Spoke

In Acts 3:16-21, Peter sets forth his central argument, based on a prophetic understanding of history. The restoration of the lame man to "perfect health" (Acts 3:16) is a sign that the messianic promises of the prophets are being fulfilled. Isaiah's prophecy of the suffering servant, in which God revealed "that his Christ should suffer" (Acts 3:18), has already been fulfilled in the Passion and death of Jesus. Hence, it is urgent that the men of Israel repent so that they may receive the promised blessing by "the faith which is through Jesus" (Acts 3:16), who will reign from heaven until the remainder of the messianic promises come to pass (Acts 3:21).

By its rejection of the Messiah, the Jerusalem establishment, "your rulers" (Acts 3:17), has turned away from God. The men of Israel must therefore depart from the course set by the Jerusalem establishment and "turn again, that [their] sins may be blotted out" (Acts 3:18). They must thus enter the messianic Israel governed by the apostles, so "that times of refreshing may come from the presence of the Lord" (Acts 3:19). There can be no doubt that Jesus is the Messiah foretold by the prophets (cf. Acts 3:20), for the apostles have witnessed His Resurrection and Ascension, just as the men of Israel have now witnessed the healing of the lame man. Beginning with the Ascension and throughout the interim period of the last days, Jesus is inaugurating His kingdom through the power of the Holy Spirit, "until the time for establishing [*apokatastáseōs*] all that God spoke by the mouth of his holy prophets" (Acts 3:21).

The term *apokatastáseōs* literally means "restoration," and the corresponding verb *apokathístēmi* ("to restore") is consistently used in the Septuagint in the context of the prophetic promise of Israel's restoration upon her return from exile. Sirach 48:10, for example, uses the term in reference to the restoration of the twelve tribes of Israel, which Jesus described as taking place through the ministry of the apostles (cf. Lk. 22:29-30). The apostles themselves use the term when asking Jesus if He will "at this time restore the kingdom to Israel" (Acts 1:6).

The Resurrection of Israel

Ezekiel depicted the restoration of Israel as a kind of corporate resurrection of the nation that would overcome the division between the northern house of Israel and the southern house of Judah (cf. Ezek. 37:1-22). Because the ten northern tribes had been thoroughly dispersed among the Gentiles, their reunion would be possible only by the incorporation of the Gentiles themselves into Israel. Hence, the restoration of Israel is nothing less than a corporate resurrection that overcomes the division between Jew and Gentile (cf. Rom. 11:15) and through which "all Israel," not only Judah, "will be saved" (Rom. 11:26). This corporate resurrection is the establishment of "all that God spoke by the mouth of his holy prophets" (Acts 3:21), an imminent fruit of the Resurrection of Jesus and a type of the eventual resurrection of the dead. The restoration of Israel was inaugurated at Pentecost and fervently pursued by the apostles during the last days before the judgment of Jerusalem. Peter is urgently concerned with

saving as many of his fellow Jews as possible before
the judgment that is to come upon the city and the
Temple, knowing that once the city is destroyed, the
Church's ministry in Judea will effectively cease.

From Abraham to the Prophets

In Acts 3:22, Peter circles back and develops his
previous argument in more detail, with particular reference to Moses and Abraham. He begins by quoting
Moses' prophecy in Deuteronomy 18:19 concerning a
future prophet:

> Moses said, "The Lord God will raise up for you a
> prophet from your brethren as he raised me up.
> You shall listen to him in whatever he tells you.
> And it shall be that every soul that does not listen
> to that prophet shall be destroyed from the people"
> (Acts 3:22-23).

Jesus, Peter declares, is this prophet like Moses
whom Moses himself foretold, and the people in
question are the People of God. Therefore, to believe
and follow Jesus is to stand in continuity with Moses
as part of the People of God. In contrast, those who,
by rejecting Jesus, refuse to "listen to" the prophet
like Moses are now cut off from the People of God
and will face judgment.[2] The restored Israel consists
of all and only those who accept and follow Jesus
as the Messiah, for He is the sign of contradiction
by whom membership in the People of God is
determined (cf. Lk. 2:34-35).

---

[2] Donald Juel, *Messianic Exegesis: Christological Interpretation of the Old
Testament in Early Christianity* (Philadelphia: Fortress Press, 1988), 84.

Peter leaves no doubt that his own time is uniquely one of prophetic fulfillment, for "all the prophets . . . proclaimed these days" (Acts 3:24), the last days of the Mosaic covenant. Through the work of the Messiah, the Mosaic covenant is being brought to its culmination, and the covenant oath sworn to Abraham, that "in your posterity shall all the families of the earth be blessed" (Acts 3:25; cf. Gen. 22:18), is being fulfilled. The Messiah has extended the blessing first to the men of Israel so that, through a penitent and reconstituted Israel, the blessing might also be offered to all the nations.[3] Thus, the Gentiles will be united to Israel in accordance with God's covenant with Abraham (cf. Gal. 3:7-9). Peter understands God's saving plan as unfolding from Abraham to Moses and all the prophets, and as reaching its fulfillment in Jesus the Messiah. The history of the People of God is the history of the covenants, converging on the New Covenant established in Christ.

The Rejected Stone

At the beginning of Acts 4, the Sadducees emerge as the chief opponents of the apostles. (The Pharisees, in contrast, had been Jesus' main antagonists during His ministry.) The Sadducees were aristocratic priests who controlled the Temple and whose economic and political interests centered on its continued operation. They adhered to a literal interpretation of the Law of Moses and rejected the Pharisees' more expansive interpretation. The Sadducees likewise rejected the

---

[3] J. Bradley Chance, *Jerusalem, the Temple, and the New Age in Luke-Acts* (Macon, Ga.: Mercer University Press, 1988), 103-4.

doctrine of the resurrection of the dead (cf. Lk. 20:27). Hence, they were doubly offended by Peter's preaching, since he both proclaimed Jesus as Messiah, whom the Sadducees had rejected, and taught the resurrection of the dead, which they regarded as absurd (cf. Acts 4:2).

As a result, the Sadducees have Peter and John arrested and brought before the high priest and other Jerusalem leaders (cf. Acts 4:3-6). When questioned about the healing of the lame man, Peter is "filled with the Holy Spirit" (Acts 4:8) and, just as Jesus had promised, is given words of "wisdom, which none of your adversaries will be able to withstand or contradict" (Lk. 21:15). Peter declares that the lame man was healed "by the name of Jesus Christ of Nazareth, whom you crucified, whom God raised from the dead" (Acts 4:10) and describes Jesus in terms of Psalm 118:22: "This is the stone which was rejected by you builders, but which has become the head of the corner" (Acts 4:11). Psalm 118:22 is a testimony that Jesus had used in His own preaching (cf. Lk. 20:17-18). In his application of the verse, Peter makes explicit what Jesus had implied subtly: The Jerusalem leaders are the "builders" who rejected Jesus, the "stone," who by His Resurrection and Ascension has become the "cornerstone" in God's new temple, the Church. Thus interpreted, Psalm 118:22 prophesies both Jesus' rejection by the Jerusalem leaders and His subsequent exaltation by God.

The Jerusalem leaders "wondered" at the "boldness" (*parrēsían*) of Peter and John (Acts 4:13). This boldness or frankness of speech is not a merely natural trait but a supernatural gift that allows the

apostles to preach courageously even in the face of
hostility. Peter's frankness is indeed remarkable con-
sidering that the leaders to whom he spoke were the
very ones who had handed over Jesus for execution
not long before and who could easily do the same to
him. Peter does not count on protection from such a
threat; he knows that some of the apostles will in fact
be put to death (cf. Lk. 21:16). Yet he is free, and his
freedom is undiminished by the danger he faces.
Physical dangers cannot touch either the life that
comes from the Holy Spirit (cf. Lk. 21:18-19) or the
gifts that come with it. The apostles' boldness corre-
sponds to the gift of fortitude, one of the seven gifts
of the Holy Spirit, which is marked by an invincible
confidence in the victory of God's will in one's life.

Peter's Prayer

Peter and John are released and return to the
disciples. Peter then leads the disciples in prayer,
employing the words of "our father David, thy servant" from the psalms (Acts 4:25). The term "servant"
has a royal connotation; in the Old Testament, it is
first and foremost the Davidic king who is the "servant" of God (cf. Ps. 89:3). Peter quotes the beginning
of Psalm 2 and applies it to Jesus, who, as the heir
of David, is now the royal "servant" (Acts 4:27).
Peter identifies the various parties mentioned in
Psalm 2:1-2 with those involved in Jesus' Crucifixion.
The "kings of the earth" correspond to Herod, the
"rulers" to Pontius Pilate, and the "peoples" with the
populace of Israel.

Psalm 2 explains that God stands with the Messiah
against their earthly enemies, including now some

from Israel. All such enemies will therefore prove to be powerless in the end. Far from thwarting God's plan of salvation, they unwittingly serve to advance that plan, which God unfolds according to His sovereign providence (cf. Acts 4:28). As a result, the disciples need not fear their opponents, but rather should face them with boldness. Accordingly, Peter prays not for relief from prosecution but for power "to speak thy word with all boldness" (Acts 4:29). His prayer for boldness is immediately heard and granted. As God shook the Temple when He revealed Himself to Isaiah (cf. Is. 6:4), He now manifests His presence to the disciples, so that "the place in which they were gathered together was shaken" (Acts 4:31). The Body of Christ constitutes a new temple that, like Solomon's Temple before it, is "filled with the Holy Spirit" (Acts 4:31).

The Dispossession of the Land

Luke describes the believers in Jerusalem as being "of one heart and soul" in their devotion to God (Acts 4:32), echoing the Deuteronomic commandment to love and serve God with all one's heart and soul. This commandment is found throughout Deuteronomy, where it is linked to the covenantal blessing of possessing the promised land: If Israel keeps the commandment, she will be blessed with possession of the land; if she disobeys, she will be cursed with its loss. Moses prophesied that, after the covenantal curses of exile and Gentile domination have come upon the Israelites, they would eventually return to God by once again loving Him with all their hearts and souls (cf. Deut. 30:1-10).

Against this background, the behavior of the believers in Jerusalem, those "of one heart and soul," provides a sharp contrast to the Deuteronomic pattern. While understanding themselves as the restored Israel, they do not seek to regain control of the land. On the contrary, "as many as were possessors of lands or houses sold them, and brought the proceeds of what was sold and laid it at the apostles' feet" (Acts 4:34-35). The dispossession of property by believers was related to the land in two ways. First, it is "lands" and "houses" that are primarily sold. Luke emphasizes this fact in the following verses when he gives the example of Barnabas, a model believer who "sold a field which belonged to him, and brought the money and laid it at the apostles' feet" (Acts 4:37). Second, it is in the environs of Jerusalem, and there alone, that the disciples sell their property. Although the growing community quickly spreads to other regions and cities, a similar practice of dispossession is not described in any of these places.

By donating the proceeds from the sale of their land to the apostles, the Jerusalem disciples acknowledge that the blessing of the New Covenant lies in the heart and soul, not in the land. Whereas life in the land was the supreme blessing of the Deuteronomic covenant, that of the New Covenant is life in the Holy Spirit, a life that is geographically universal. The land and the city of Jerusalem stood under an impending judgment and could no longer serve as a source of covenantal blessing. Far from clinging to these ancient symbols of national identity, the disciples in Jerusalem watched and prayed, knowing that the day would soon come when they would have to flee (cf. Lk. 21:20-22).

Questions for Discussion

1. Peter alludes to Isaiah's suffering servant in Acts 3:13-14. Read Isaiah 52:1-12 (concerning the new exodus) and 52:13–53:12 (concerning the suffering servant).

a. How does the suffering servant bring about the new exodus?

_____

_____

b. What does Isaiah's description tell us about the ministry of Christ?

_____

_____

2. Read Acts 3:24, where Peter teaches that the Old Testament prophets looked forward to the restoration of Israel in the New Covenant. How do the teachings of the prophets shape our understanding of the Church?

_____

_____

3. Acts 4:2 refers to the apostles' teaching on the resurrection of the dead. Read Catechism, nos. 994-95 and 1019.

a. Why is the bodily resurrection of the dead central to the Catholic faith?

_____

_____

b. How does the resurrection of the dead relate to the Resurrection of Jesus?

_____

_____

4. Read Catechism, nos. 1002-3. How do the Sacraments of Baptism and the Eucharist prepare the believer for the coming resurrection?

_____

_____

5. In Acts 4:11, Peter compares Jesus to the stone of Psalm 118:22. Read Psalm 118. In what sense is Jesus the stone that was rejected?

_____

_____

6. Read Acts 4:13, where the Jerusalem leaders wonder at Peter and John's "boldness" in preaching to them. How do we use the graces given to us in the Sacraments of Baptism and Confirmation to proclaim with boldness the teaching of Jesus and the truths of the faith?

_____

_____

7. Read Psalm 2 and Acts 4:25-28. How does Peter apply this psalm to Jesus?

_____

_____

8. Read Acts 4:32. How do the disciples in Jerusalem fulfill the greatest commandment of the Deuteronomic covenant (cf. Mk. 12:28-30), even as they transcend that covenant?

_____

_____

6

THE WITNESS OF STEPHEN
—ACTS 6-7—

In Acts 6, Luke describes the first episode of tension within the rapidly growing community of disciples: "[T]he Hellenists murmured against the Hebrews because their widows were neglected in the daily distribution [*diakoniai*]" (Acts 6:1). The Hellenists were Jews whose first language was Greek, while the "Hebrews" were Jews whose first language was Aramaic. The Hellenists consisted largely of Jews from the Diaspora who had repatriated to Jerusalem for religious reasons (cf. Acts 2:5; 6:9). Many of them had come to faith in Jesus in response to Peter's sermon on Pentecost (cf. Acts 2:41).

The Service of the Seven

The synagogues of Jerusalem, which many of the disciples continued to attend, were divided according to the language in which services were conducted. The existence of these separate Hellenist and Hebrew synagogues was at the root of the neglect of the Hellenists' widows. The apostles, as Aramaic speakers, had less regular contact with the Greek-speaking disciples, allowing situations of need to be overlooked inadvertently. Having become aware of the problem, the apostles acted promptly to correct it (cf. Acts 6:2-3).

The solution was to select from among the Hellenists seven men who were charged with administering the daily distribution, a large and important ministry in a community that by this time

may have numbered in the tens of thousands.
The apostles refer to this ministry as a calling "to
serve [*diakoneîn*] tables" (Acts 6:2). The phrase "to
serve tables" is not so much a description of the
physical activity involved as it is a reflection of
Jesus' teaching on leadership as service.[1] At the Last
Supper, Jesus taught:

> [L]et the greatest among you become as the
> youngest, and the leader as one who serves
> [*diakonôn*]. For which is the greater, one who sits at
> table, or one who serves [*diakonôn*]? Is it not the one
> who sits at table? But I am among you as one who
> serves [*diakonôn*] (Lk. 22:26-27).

The apostles were not merely appointing the seven
to an administrative task but were giving them a
share in their leadership within the Church. Hence,
the seven are ordained to the diaconate by the laying
on of hands (cf. Acts 6:6), the same ritual action that
was used in the ordination of Levites (cf. Num. 8:10).

The Preaching of Stephen

The seven also served as evangelizers (cf. Acts
8:5), and the most prominent among them was
Stephen (cf. Acts 6:8). Whereas Peter regularly
preached in the Temple (cf. Acts 5:42), Stephen was
the first disciple to preach in the synagogues, as Paul
was later to make his usual practice. Such preaching
required great boldness on Stephen's part, as the

---

[1] J. Bradley Chance, *Jerusalem, the Temple, and the New Age in Luke-Acts*
(Macon, Ga.: Mercer University Press, 1988), 107.

Jerusalem synagogues were the strongholds of the Pharisees, and, indeed, Stephen was remembered as a man "full of grace and power" (Acts 6:8).

Opposition to Stephen's preaching arose among the unconverted Hellenists of the "synagogue of the Freedmen" (Acts 6:9). As Jews who had chosen to return to Jerusalem from the Diaspora, the Hellenists tended to be more rigoristic than the Aramaic speakers in their devotion to the Temple and their interpretation of the Deuteronomic Law. Jesus had strongly criticized the leaders of the Temple cult (cf. Lk. 19:45-46; 20:9-19; 21:5-6). When preaching among the Hellenists, Stephen had evidently repeated Jesus' criticisms, thereby engendering fierce opposition.

Luke relates that the synagogue of the Freedmen included members from the province of Cilicia in southeast Asia Minor (cf. Acts 6:9), where Tarsus was located. Given the subsequent role of Saul of Tarsus in the stoning of Stephen (cf. Acts 7:58), Saul was evidently a member of the synagogue of the Freedmen and a leader of those who brought charges against Stephen. Ironically, Saul would have very similar experiences with the Hellenists after his conversion: When he preaches among them, they try to kill him (cf. Acts 9:28-29). Later, they bring the same charges against him that they had brought against Stephen (cf. Acts 21:27-28).

Stephen is seized by the Hellenists and brought before the Sanhedrin (cf. Acts 6:12). In contrast to the previous arrests of Peter and John, the Sadducees are not mentioned among Stephen's opponents (cf. Acts 6:12), an absence consistent with the opposition to

Stephen coming from the Hellenist synagogues. Stephen is charged by "false witnesses" (Acts 6:13) with preaching "that this Jesus of Nazareth will destroy this place [the Temple], and will change the customs which Moses delivered to us" (Acts 6:14). The witnesses against Stephen are false in the same sense that those who testified against Jesus had been false (cf. Mk. 14:57-58). Their charges were not entirely fabricated, but they misrepresented Jesus' message. Jesus had prophesied that the Jews themselves would bring about the destruction of the Temple through their corruption of its cult and their rejection of the Messiah (cf. Jn. 2:19; Lk. 21:5-6); He did not say that He Himself would destroy it.

Land, Law, and Temple

When the High Priest asks Stephen to answer the charges against him (cf. Acts 7:1), his response before the Sanhedrin is extraordinary. He does not expressly deny the charges but instead, in the longest speech in the Book of Acts, vigorously defends his previous preaching as the true faith of Israel. His speech is strongly grounded in the earlier preaching of Peter, which centered on the fulfillment of the covenant through the Messiah's deliverance of Israel from the Deuteronomic curses. The speech is constructed around an interpretive retelling of the history of the People of God drawn from the Old Testament.[2] Paul will later employ the same technique in his sermons (e.g., Acts 13:16-25). Stephen's

---

[2] Craig A. Evans and James A. Sanders, *Luke and Scripture: The Function of Sacred Tradition in Luke-Acts* (Minneapolis: Fortress Press, 1993), 194.

interpretation of Israel's failings is not novel, but rather is closely drawn from that of the prophets.[3]

The speech centers on three facets of the Deuteronomic covenant: the promised land, the Law, and the Temple. Stephen suggests that Israel's lapses into apostasy, far from being transient aberrations, are rooted in her idolatrous attitude toward these facets of the covenant. In sharp contrast to many of the Hellenist Jews, Stephen views the condition of being outside the land as neutral with respect to covenantal relation with God: God is everywhere and therefore can receive worship and bestow His blessings anywhere. Conversely, the Deuteronomic curses can be afflicted even within the land, as they now are in the form of bondage to the Romans. Stephen thus develops the universalism of the prophets into a fully Catholic perspective. His speech is therefore foundational for Christian inter-pretation of the Old Testament, and, following his martyrdom, his theology had a profound effect on the development of the Church.

Stephen's Speech

Stephen's speech can be divided into four parts. The first part (Acts 7:2-5) relates to Israel's Abrahamic identity, the second (Acts 7:6-19) to the covenantal curses, the third (Acts 7:20-40) to Israel's rejection of her deliverers, and the fourth (Acts 7:41-53) to the prophetic critique of the Temple cult.

---

[3] Rebecca I. Denova, *The Things Accomplished Among Us: Prophetic Tradition in the Structural Pattern of Luke-Acts*, Journal for the Study of the New Testament Supplement Series, vol. 141 (Sheffield, England: Sheffield Academic Press, 1997), 161.

Stephen begins by recounting Abraham's calling and journey to the promised land (cf. Acts 7:2-4). Abraham received the "covenant of circumcision" because of his faith in God's promises (Acts 7:8). The disciples, unlike Stephen's accusers, share the faith of Abraham and are thus the true sons of the patriarch (cf. Lk. 3:8; 13:28). By pointing out that God appeared to Abraham in Mesopotamia (cf. Acts 7:2), Stephen shows that God's presence is not limited to Judah, much less to the Temple. He thereby sets the stage for his critique of the Temple cult. Stephen notes that Abraham never possessed the promised land, "not even a foot's length" (Acts 7:5), underscoring that Abraham was in covenant with God without the land.

Stephen next refers to Israel's exile and bondage in Egypt (cf. Acts 7:6), a condition that foreshadowed the Jews' bondage under the Romans in his own day. The sons of Israel sold Joseph into slavery in Egypt, "but God was with him," even though he was outside the land (Acts 7:9). Though the sons of Israel had rejected Joseph out of jealousy, God had appointed him to be their deliverer. Joseph thus saved his people in spite of their hostility towards him (cf. Acts 7:11-14).

Moses experienced a similar pattern of hostility: "He supposed that his brethren understood that God was giving them deliverance by his hand, but they did not understand" (Acts 7:25). Though God had sent Moses "as both ruler and deliverer" (Acts 7:35), the Israelites rejected him, just as their ancestors had rejected Joseph and their descendants would reject Jesus. The same Moses who received the Law on Mount Sinai (cf. Acts 7:38) also foretold the coming of a prophet like himself (cf. Acts 7:37), that is, a lawgiver and covenant maker. Stephen, like Peter, teaches that Jesus is this prophet (cf. Acts 3:22). Therefore, to obey the word of Moses, one must now follow Jesus. Only thus can one remain "in the congregation [*ekklēsíai*]" of the People of God (Acts 7:38). The Mosaic Law is not a closed system, a completed revelation given on Mount Sinai for all time, as the Pharisees and the Sadducees thought. On the contrary, the Mosaic Law points beyond itself from within itself.

The Israelites "refused to obey" Moses and "thrust him aside" (Acts 7:39), instead choosing to fashion a golden calf for their worship (cf. Acts 7:40-41). This act of apostasy led to the wandering of the wilderness generation, which Stephen sees as a type of his contemporaries, just as Moses is a type of Jesus. The cause of the Israelites' apostasy was their idolatrous preference for "the works of their hands" (Acts 7:41) over the unfamiliar gift of God. The same idolatrous attitude, Stephen suggests, has now infected the Temple cult.

Quoting the prophet Amos's condemnation of the wilderness generation, Stephen warns his contemporaries not to repeat the error of their ancestors (cf. Acts 7:42-43; Amos 5:25-27). The Israelites engaged in idolatry in the wilderness even after they had been given the tabernacle containing the ark of the covenant, which God had directed Moses to make "according to the pattern that he had seen" on Mount Sinai (Acts 7:44). The tabernacle was brought into the promised land by Joshua and was eventually brought to Jerusalem by David, who sought "to find a habitation for the God of Jacob" (Acts 7:46). David's ardent desire to relocate the tabernacle to Jerusalem is celebrated in Psalm 132, to which Stephen alludes: "I will not give sleep to my eyes or slumber to my eyelids, until I find a place for the LORD, a dwelling place for the Mighty One of Jacob" (Ps. 132:4-5). David eventually succeeded in relocating the tabernacle, as described in 2 Samuel 6:1-17.

Many years later, Solomon constructed the Temple as a "house" for God (Acts 7:47). Yet, Stephen notes sharply, the presence of God is not limited to "houses made with hands [*cheiropoiētois*]" (Acts 7:48). The Greek term *cheiropoiētos* is distinctive in that it is used in the Septuagint exclusively for pagan shrines. Thus, Stephen is tacitly accusing his audience of holding an idolatrous attitude toward the Temple. Both the Hellenist Jews and the Jerusalem authorities have betrayed Israel's mission to serve as a light to the nations, instead making the Temple a center of ethnic privilege.

Stephen's critique of the Temple cult is no innovation, but is drawn from that of the prophets, as he shows with his quotation of Isaiah 66:1-2 (cf. Acts 7:49-50). Isaiah's oracle asserts that God has created the cosmos itself as His "house," and therefore no structure built by man can be adequate to contain Him. Solomon had made this very point at the dedication of the Temple (cf. 1 Kings 8:27) but prayed that God would nevertheless use the Temple to bless His people. However, Isaiah foresaw in his oracle a time when such would not be the case, and the corruption of the Temple cult would reduce its sacrifices to the status of idolatry.

> He who slaughters an ox is like him who kills a man;
> he who sacrifices a lamb, like him who breaks a
> dog's neck; he who presents a cereal offering, like
> him who offers swine's blood; he who makes a
> memorial offering of frankincense, like him who
> blesses an idol (Is. 66:3).

Such a time of corruption, Stephen implies, has
arrived. By placing their faith in a Temple built by
man as though it alone contained the presence of
God, his accusers have preferred the work of human
hands to God Himself.

Uncircumcised Hearts

At the end of his speech, Stephen describes his
audience as "uncircumcised in heart" like their fathers
(Acts 7:51) and thus not truly sons of Abraham.
Stephen's charge employs traditional prophetic
language (cf. Jer. 9:25-26) that is ultimately drawn
from Deuteronomy 30:1-6. Moses prophesied that one
day God would "circumcise your heart and the heart
of your offspring, so that you will love the LORD your
God with all your heart and with all your soul, that
you may live" (Deut. 30:6).

Deuteronomy 30:1-6 concerns Israel's eventual
deliverance from the Deuteronomic curses, which
come upon the Israelites because they "resist the Holy
Spirit" (Acts 7:51). Their resistance is not merely
passive but has often expressed itself in murderous
violence; Stephen asks, "Which of the prophets did
not your fathers persecute?" (Acts 7:52). The prophets
foretold a new covenant not like the Mosaic covenant
(Jer. 31:31-32), but the Israelites rejected the prophets,
as now their descendants reject the Messiah.

Stephen's speech reaches its climax with the Messiah, in whom the ministry of the prophets attains its completion. Although the Hellenists have accused Stephen of speaking "blasphemous words against Moses and God" (Acts 6:11), their actions have ironically shown themselves to be guilty of such blasphemy. As their fathers "killed those who announced beforehand the coming of the Righteous One," the Messiah, so they "have now betrayed and murdered" the Messiah Himself (Acts 7:52; cf. 3:14-15). Stephen's opponents, unlike the disciples of Jesus, are not true sons of Abraham, for they have rejected the Messiah, who alone circumcises the heart through the Holy Spirit, (cf. Acts 7:51). The gift of the Spirit is the culmination of the Law and the Prophets and even now works to restore Israel and deliver her from the Deuteronomic curses. Stephen's accusers, however, have not accepted the Law and the Prophets they profess (cf. Acts 7:53) but have rejected the God of the Scriptures and His Messiah.

The Vindication of the Son of Man

By the time Stephen has completed his speech, his audience is "enraged, and they ground their teeth against him" (Acts 7:54). Stephen sees their rage and realizes the imminent danger he faces, but his mind is not occupied by his earthly fate. Rather, "full of the Holy Spirit," he "gazed into heaven and saw the glory of God" (Acts 7:55). Jesus ascended into the cloud of glory, and from the Ascension onward dwells within that glory "at the right hand of God" (Acts 7:55). Stephen's vision reveals that Jesus, a man whom the

Sanhedrin condemned to death, is now alive and sharing in the divine glory. At His own trial, Jesus prophesied that "from now on the Son of man shall be seated at the right hand of the power of God" (Lk. 22:69), and the Sanhedrin had denounced His words as blasphemy (cf. Lk. 22:71). Stephen's vision confirms Jesus' prophecy and thus, from the Sanhedrin's perspective, adds a second "blasphemy" to that of Jesus. The scandal of Stephen's "blasphemy" is intensified by the fact that, through his speech, he has claimed that Jesus' place as the exalted Messiah is established within, and in no way against, the strict monotheism of the Law and the Prophets.

Stephen declares to the Sanhedrin, "Behold, I see the heavens opened, and the Son of man standing at the right hand of God" (Acts 7:56). This declaration is the only passage in Acts in which the title "Son of man" is used and one of the few examples of its use in the New Testament by someone other than Jesus Himself. Stephen's declaration, like Jesus' prophecy, is a combined reference to Psalm 110:1 and Daniel 7:13. In the former, the son of David is exalted at the "right hand" of God, while in the latter, "one like a son of man" comes from earth to the throne of God, signifying his vindication by God. Thus, Stephen's declaration identifies Jesus as the exalted Messiah and the Son of man vindicated in heaven, while implying His impending vindication on earth. The Ascension inaugurated the presence of Jesus' humanity in heaven, from which He reigns in glory. Stephen now testifies to the manifestation of that presence on earth, as the kingdom of God breaks into the earthly realm.

The Martyrdom of Stephen

The Sanhedrin never renders a judgment on Stephen. Rather, the enraged witnesses—the Hellenists who brought the charges against him—take the law into their own hands and seize him (cf. Acts 7:57). Thus, after they have "cast him out of the city" in order to stone him, "the witnesses," not the members of the Sanhedrin, "laid down their garments at the feet of a young man named Saul" (Acts 7:58). Placing their garments "at the feet" of Saul indicates his leadership of the group. As Stephen is being stoned, he cries out in the first prayer recorded in Acts that is explicitly addressed to Jesus: "Lord Jesus, receive my spirit" (Acts 7:59).

Stephen is the only disciple whose martyrdom Luke describes in detail, and, like Jesus on the Cross, Stephen prays for the forgiveness of his murders: "Lord, do not hold this sin against them" (Acts 7:60). Stephen's prayer of forgiveness indicates that in spite of the ferocity of the persecution, the proper attitude of the disciple is one of forgiveness. Yet, an attitude of forgiveness does not imply that such persecution is without consequences. On the contrary, the murder of Stephen conforms to the prophetic warning of Jesus:

> [T]he Wisdom of God said, "I will send them prophets and apostles, some of whom they will kill and persecute," that the blood of all the prophets, shed from the foundation of the world, may be required of this generation, from the blood of Abel to the blood of Zechariah, who perished between the altar and the sanctuary. Yes, I tell you, it shall be required of this generation (Lk. 11:49-51).

The death of Stephen initiated a period of persistent and widespread persecution (cf. Acts 8:1), the first the Church would suffer. This period was brought to a close only by the destruction of Jerusalem by the Romans in A.D. 70.

*   *   *

Questions for Discussion

1. Read Acts 6:2-3. How does the diaconate carry on today the mission described in this passage?

_____

_____

2. Stephen exhibited great boldness in preaching in a hostile environment.

a. How might we prudently seek opportunities to evangelize, even when we might suffer personal discomfort or encounter hostility?

_____

_____

_____

b. How does the gift of fortitude, one of the seven gifts of the Holy Spirit, enable us to persevere in such situations?

_____

_____

c. Do we pray for an increase in the gift of fortitude in order to strengthen our apostolic work?

_____

3. Stephen encountered his greatest opposition from within the Hellenist synagogue of which he himself was a member.

a. Do faithful Catholics sometimes meet opposition from those who ought to be most supportive of their efforts?

_____

_____

b. Read Acts 7:60. How does Stephen's attitude of perfect forgiveness serve as a model for us in such painful situations?

_____

_____

c. What are some circumstances in which we must pray for and forgive those who misunderstand and malign us?

_____

_____

4. Stephen emphasizes that the Law and the Prophets point beyond themselves to the Messiah who fulfills them. Read Catechism, nos. 121-23.

a. Why is an interpretation of the Law and the Prophets that rejects Jesus Christ necessarily a false interpretation?

_____

_____

b. How should this Christian understanding of the Law and the Prophets shape our reading of the Old Testament?

_____

_____

5. Read Deuteronomy 18:15; Luke 7:16; 13:33; and 24:19; and Acts 3:22 and 7:37. How is Jesus the prophet like Moses?

_____

_____

6. Compare Acts 4:8-12, 24-30 to Acts 7:47-53. How does Stephen's preaching draw on and develop that of Peter?

_____

_____

7

FROM JUDEA TO SAMARIA
—ACTS 8-9—

The murder of Stephen marked the beginning of a campaign of persecution against the Church in Jerusalem, primarily targeting the Hellenist disciples who had been close to the martyr.[1] Saul of Tarsus was a leading organizer of the persecution (cf. Acts 8:3). He was highly effective in this endeavor and sought not only to imprison the disciples but also to put them to death. By his own testimony, his goal was no less than to destroy the Church (cf. Gal. 1:13). Ironically, the immediate effect of the persecution is to induce the scattered disciples to go "about preaching the word" throughout Judea and Samaria (Acts 8:4), demonstrating that God is sovereign and employs even the opposition of men to fulfill His salvific plan.

Among the Samaritans

The apostles remain in Jerusalem in spite of the persecution, but the surviving Hellenist deacons are forced to flee. Among the deacons, Philip takes advantage of his flight, using it as an opportunity to preach the Gospel in Samaria (cf. Acts 8:5). In doing so, Philip initiates the second part of the itinerary through which the Risen Christ had commanded the apostles to "restore the kingdom to Israel" (Acts 1:6):

[Y]ou shall receive power when the Holy Spirit has come upon you; and you shall be my witnesses in

---

[1] F. F. Bruce, *New Testament History* (Garden City, N.Y.: Doubleday & Company, 1969), 226.

> Jerusalem and in all Judea and Samaria and to the
> end of the earth (Acts 1:8).

The emphasis placed on "Judea and Samaria" is the result of the historic division of the kingdom of David. While Judea was home to the southern tribes of Judah and Benjamin, Samaria contained the mixed remnant of the ten northern tribes. Hence, it is imperative that the Gospel be preached in Samaria as well as Judea, so that all twelve tribes can be united under the apostles in a restored kingdom.

Philip proclaims to the Samaritans not only the kingdom of God, but also Jesus as the messianic king in whom the kingdom has come (cf. Acts 8:5, 12). The Samaritans looked forward to a prophet like Moses (cf. Deut. 18:15-19), with whom Peter and Stephen had identified Jesus in their preaching (cf. Acts 3:22-23; 7:37). The Samaritans, perhaps in light of this Deuteronomic expectation, readily "believed Philip as he preached good news" and "were baptized" (Acts 8:12). As soon as the apostles in Jerusalem hear of the Samaritan converts, Peter and John go to Samaria to confirm the new disciples in the Holy Spirit (cf. Acts 8:14-17). Thus, the apostles exercise their ministry in a universal manner, without geographic or ethnic limitation, thereby effecting and demonstrating the unity of the People of God. In Christ, there is neither Jew nor Samaritan, but all are members of Israel restored under the son of David. The reunion of the twelve tribes is brought about by the Holy Spirit, who achieves what centuries of political and military maneuvering by Judea had failed to achieve.

Samaria had long been home to various syncretic sects that mixed forms of Hellenistic paganism with the religion of Israel. According to the Church Fathers, Simon Magus was the leader of one such group and taught a kind of proto-Gnosticism.[2] Luke reports that Simon was also a great practitioner of magic (cf. Acts 8:9, 11). After hearing Philip preach, Simon believes, is baptized, and begins to travel with Philip (cf. Acts 8:13). However, upon seeing Peter and John confirming the Samaritans, "he offered them money, saying 'Give me also this power'" (Acts 8:19). Simon had evidently not truly repented of his previous way of life or patterns of thought. He understood the gift of the Spirit as only another form of magic that he might add to his repertoire. Peter therefore pronounces a condemnation upon Simon for the wicked "intent of [his] heart" (Acts 8:22).

Isaiah and the Eunuch

From Samaria, the Holy Spirit presses Philip onward, directing him to join an Ethiopian eunuch, probably a Jewish proselyte, whom he finds reading a passage from the prophet Isaiah (cf. Acts 8:29-30):

As a sheep led to the slaughter or a lamb before its shearer is dumb, so he opens not his mouth. In his humiliation justice was denied him. Who can describe his generation? For his life is taken up from the earth (Acts 8:32-33; cf. Is. 53:7-8).

---

[2] Cf. St. Justin Martyr, *First Apology*, chap. 26; St. Irenaeus, *Against Heresies*, bk. I, chap. 23.

When asked if he understands what he is reading, the eunuch replies, "How can I, unless some one guides me?" (Acts 8:31). The eunuch's response conveys the profound truth that Scripture does not interpret itself, but rather must be interpreted in light of the Tradition handed on by Jesus to the apostles. Countless learned Jews had studied Isaiah 53:7-8 without comprehending its application to the messianic work of Jesus. The passage refers to one who allows himself to be offered up as a sacrificial lamb and does not speak in his own defense, whose death is unjust, but who is "taken up from the earth." Philip explains the passage in reference to Jesus' rejection and Passion, followed by His Resurrection and Ascension, which vindicate His messianic status.[3]

At the eunuch's request, Philip baptizes him (cf. Acts 8:36-38), which ironically fulfills another prophecy in Isaiah:

> For thus says the LORD: "To the eunuchs who keep my sabbaths, who choose the things that please me and hold fast my covenant, I will give in my house and within my walls a monument and a name better than sons and daughters; I will give them an everlasting name which shall not be cut off" (Is. 56:4-5).

Isaiah's prophecy of the eunuchs' coming to God is immediately followed by another concerning the

---

[3] Donald Juel, *Messianic Exegesis: Christological Interpretation of the Old Testament in Early Christianity* (Philadelphia: Fortress Press, 1988), 128; Craig A. Evans and James A. Sanders, *Luke and Scripture: The Function of Sacred Tradition in Luke-Acts* (Minneapolis: Fortress Press, 1993), 201-2.

foreigners who do so as well (cf. Is. 56:6-8). Thus, the baptism of the Ethiopian eunuch serves as a prelude to the baptism of the first Gentile by Peter (cf. Acts 10).

The Zeal of Saul

Meanwhile, as the disciples fan out from Jerusalem, Saul decides to pursue them. The Romans had given the high priest a certain degree of legal authority over Jews living outside of Judea, and Saul is able to obtain from him warrants for the arrest of any Jewish disciples in Damascus (cf. Acts 9:1-2). Damascus was the first city on the road from Jerusalem to Babylon, where the largest population of Jews in the Diaspora lived. Since Damascus itself had a sizable population of Jews, it was a logical place for Saul to begin his work of "threats and murder" (Acts 9:1).

As a Pharisee, Saul believed that the Deuteronomic covenant had been violated by Israel, bringing upon her the Deuteronomic curses, including oppression by Gentiles. He feared that deviation from the Deuteronomic Law would bring further divine punishment and sought strict observance of the Law in order to repair the covenant. Only when Israel had become holy through observance of the Law would God send the Messiah to restore the kingdom. The most rigorous Pharisees held that even violence should be employed to prevent deviation from the Law and looked to biblical examples like Phineas, whose zeal for the Law led him to kill a Hebrew man and his Midianite wife (cf. Num. 25:6-13). The readiness to employ violence for such a purpose was considered a mark of zeal, and it was to such zeal that Paul would later attribute his efforts to destroy the Church (cf. Phil. 3:5-6; Gal. 1:13-14). From Saul's perspective, the followers of Jesus were disloyal to the Deuteronomic covenant and thereby impeded the coming of the Messiah. Zeal therefore demanded that the disciples be eliminated. Of course, Saul's perspective rested on the assumption that Jesus was not truly the Messiah. Once that assumption was reversed, Saul's world was turned upside down.

The Messiah Revealed

On the road to Damascus, Saul sees a great light from heaven (cf. Acts 9:3). Isaiah had spoken of the great light that would accompany the redemption of the lands of the northernmost tribes, the first to have been conquered by the Assyrians.

> In the former time he brought into contempt the land of Zebulun and the land of Naphtali, but in the latter time he will make glorious the way of the sea, the land beyond the Jordan, Galilee of the nations. The people who walked in darkness have seen a great light; those who dwelt in a land of deep darkness, on them has light shined (Is. 9:1-2).

The road to Damascus on which Saul was traveling passed through the tribal land of Zebulun.[4] Saul hears

---

[4] Rainer Riesner, *Paul's Early Period: Chronology, Mission Strategy, Theology*, trans. Doug Stott (Grand Rapids: William B. Eerdmans Publishing Company, 1998), 237-40.

a voice say to him, "Saul, Saul, why do you persecute me?" (Acts 9:4). Paul will later derive his understanding of the Church as the Body of Christ from these words. Saul had been persecuting the disciples of Christ, but Christ asked him, "[W]hy do you persecute *me*?" (emphasis added). To persecute the Church is to persecute Christ, for the Church is the Mystical Body of Christ.

In a state of confusion, Saul asks, "Who are you, Lord?" and the speaker reveals Himself to be the resurrected and ascended Jesus (Acts 9:5). Saul now knows that the apostles' proclamation of Jesus as risen from the dead is true. Because of His Crucifixion, Jesus had appeared to be a false Messiah, but His Resurrection and Ascension prove that He is the true Messiah. Saul had believed that the general resurrection of the dead would occur before the restoration of Israel. Instead, the Resurrection of Jesus alone had occurred before the restoration of Israel, inaugurating the kingdom for those who would enter it. Saul had misinterpreted the Law and the Prophets, just as Stephen had charged. Though Saul had helped put Stephen to death, he now realizes that Stephen was right. Stephen's understanding of the Law would become a core element of Paul's teaching.

Saul Between Worlds

When Saul arises from the ground, he is blind. His physical blindness symbolizes and impresses upon him the spiritual blindness from which he has long suffered. Jesus had used this very metaphor in connection with the Pharisees.

Jesus said, "For judgment I came into this world, that those who do not see may see, and that those who see may become blind." Some of the Pharisees near him heard this, and they said to him, "Are we also blind?" Jesus said to them, "If you were blind, you would have no guilt; but now that you say, 'We see,' your guilt remains" (Jn. 9:39-41).

Jesus instructs a disciple in Damascus named Ananias, "a devout man according to the law, well spoken of by all the Jews who lived there" (Acts 22:12), to seek out Saul. Ananias protests, referring to Saul's persecution of the Church:

Lord, I have heard from many about this man, how much evil he has done to thy saints at Jerusalem; and here he has authority from the chief priests to bind all who call upon thy name (Acts 9:13-14).

It is noteworthy that Ananias already has knowledge not only of Saul's activity in Jerusalem, but also of his plans for Damascus. The Church did not survive and rapidly grow in the face of fierce persecution through ignorance or indifference towards her enemies.

Jesus nevertheless commands Ananias to go to Saul, "for he is a chosen instrument of mine to carry my name before the Gentiles and kings and the sons of Israel" (Acts 9:15). Neither here nor elsewhere in Acts is there any indication that Paul's impending ministry will be limited to the Gentiles. Rather, Paul will be given a prophetic mission to both the Gentiles and to all Israel concerning "the promise made by God to our fathers, to which our twelve tribes hope to attain" (Acts 26:6-7). The present necessity, however, is for Saul to submit to the representative of the

Church, through whom his sight is restored and he is baptized (cf. Acts 9:17-18).

On his first visit to Jerusalem, Saul is spurned by the disciples there, who remember his persecution of the Church only too well. Only the intervention of Barnabas, who had knowledge of Saul's experience in Damascus (cf. Acts 9:27), brings the ostracism of Saul to an end. Barnabas is the name given by the apostles to Joseph the Levite (cf. Acts 4:36), a disciple whom the apostles greatly respected. Barnabas intercedes with the apostles and opens the way for Saul to stay with Peter for fifteen days (cf. Gal. 1:18). However, when Saul begins preaching to the Hellenists, he encounters the same opposition as had Stephen. The Hellenists begin plotting to kill Saul, but Saul returns to Tarsus after the brethren warn him to flee (cf. Acts 9:29-30).

The Vicar of Christ

Luke describes how Peter begins the practice of making pastoral visitations to the scattered communities of disciples, going "here and there among them all" (Acts 9:32). During these visitations, Peter heals the sick and even raises the dead (cf. Acts 9:33-42), just as Jesus did during His messianic ministry. Hence, Peter visibly represents Jesus through these visitations, extending the earthly ministry of Jesus into the present time. It is on one such pastoral visitation that Peter will be led by the Holy Spirit to evangelize and baptize the first Gentile converts.

* * *

Questions for Discussion

1. Read Catechism, nos. 813-16. In our age, many secular ideologies seek to overcome ethnic differences and unite mankind.

a. How does the Catholic faith bring about such unity?

_____

_____

b. What is the role of the Holy Spirit in bringing about unity through the Body of Christ?

_____

_____

2. Read Acts 8:1-4, which describes the persecution of the Church in Jerusalem.

a. Two centuries after Christ, Tertullian said that "the blood of the martyrs is the seed of the Church." How was this adage true in the days of the apostles?

_____

_____

b. How does this principle still apply today?

_____

_____

3. The knowledge that Jesus is truly risen from the dead brought about a radical change in Saul's understanding of God's plan for mankind.

a. How does the Resurrection of Jesus distinguish Christianity from every other form of monotheism?

_____

_____

b. Read 1 Corinthians 15:14. Why does Paul place the Resurrection at the center of the Catholic faith?

_____

_____

4. Read Acts 9:13-17. Despite his fear, Ananias faithfully obeys Christ's command to go to Saul.

a. How can we bear witness to Christ among those who are hostile or indifferent to the faith?

_____

_____

b. Which spiritual works of mercy can we perform for those whom we do not like or with whom we have little in common?

_____

_____

8

THE ABOLITION OF SEPARATION
—ACTS 10-11—

I n Acts 10-11, Luke describes a series of events that were pivotal for the rapidly growing Church. The Jewish disciples were forcefully confronted with the question of whether it was permissible for them to eat foods declared unclean by the Deuteronomic Law. The answer to this question would determine whether the disciples could share in table fellowship with the uncircumcised, who were not within the Deuteronomic covenant. Table fellowship was a particular concern of the Pharisees, who strictly regulated it so as to enforce separation from the unclean Gentile world. No fewer than 229 of the 341 rabbinic texts in the Mishnah, a compilation of Jewish traditions that dates from A.D. 200 and is attributed to the Pharisees, concern the regulation of table fellowship.[1] A Pharisee was identified largely by the manner and the company in which he ate.

The question of unclean foods and table fellowship was immediately related to a second question that was posed to the disciples: Can the uncircumcised be baptized? The latter question follows from the first because Baptism admits one to Eucharistic communion, the most intimate form of fellowship. Through the actions and teaching of Peter, both questions are answered clearly in the affirmative. Baptism grants entry to the New Covenant, which is governed, not by the Deuteronomic Law, but by the New Law, the

---

[1] Marcus J. Borg, *Conflict, Holiness, and Politics in the Teachings of Jesus* (Harrisburg: Trinity Press International, 1998), 95.

law of the Spirit (cf. Rom. 8:2). The New Covenant creates a single People of God, embracing both Jew and Gentile: Israel restored by the Messiah through the Holy Spirit.

The New Temple

Luke describes the Gentile mission as beginning with an encounter between Peter and a Roman centurion named Cornelius, "a devout man who feared God with all his household" (Acts 10:2). The God-fearers were Gentiles who, while not converting fully to Judaism and becoming proselytes, nevertheless believed in and worshipped the God of Israel. Cornelius receives a vision from an angel at "the ninth hour of the day" (Acts 10:3), the hour at which the evening sacrifice is conducted in the Temple. The angel tells Cornelius that his prayers and alms "have ascended as a memorial before God" (Acts 10:4). The terminology of the ascending memorial is used in Leviticus to describe the fragrance of the burnt sacrificial offering rising to God (Lev. 2:2, 9; 6:15). Hence, the angel's message signifies that although he is a Gentile, Cornelius' prayer and alms have been accepted by God in place of the Temple sacrifices that would be offered by a Jew. The angel's words thus foreshadow the incorporation of the Gentiles into the new temple of the Body of Christ, fulfilling Isaiah's prophecy:

> And the foreigners who join themselves to the LORD, to minister to him, to love the name of the LORD, and to be his servants, every one who keeps the sabbath, and does not profane it, and holds fast my covenant—these I will bring to my holy mountain,

and make them joyful in my house of prayer; their burnt offerings and their sacrifices will be accepted on my altar; for my house shall be called a house of prayer for all peoples. Thus says the Lord GOD, who gathers the outcasts of Israel, I will gather yet others to him besides those already gathered (Is. 56:6-8).

The angel then instructs Cornelius to "send men to Joppa, and bring one Simon who is called Peter" (Acts 10:5).

Cleansing the World

On the following day, as Cornelius' men approach Joppa, Peter receives a vision in which God instructs him to kill and eat "all kinds of animals and reptiles and birds of the air" (Acts 10:12-13), including those declared unclean and prohibited for eating in the Deuteronomic Law. Peter protests that he has "never eaten anything that is common or unclean" (Acts 10:14), only to be told that "[w]hat God has cleansed, you must not call common" (Acts 10:15). The concept of the "unclean," first described in Leviticus 10 and developed in detail in Leviticus 11-15, is central to the Deuteronomic Law (cf. Deut. 14:3-20). The concept does not pertain to moral evil, but rather to a symbolic representation of physical evil. In particular, those things are unclean that reflect the fallenness of the world. Throughout Leviticus and Deuteronomy, the concern is to segregate Israel symbolically from the fallenness of the world in order to protect her fragile spiritual fitness to enter the presence of God in worship. The criterion of cleanness thus regulates access to the Temple. Similarly, the term "common" refers to what is unfit for the Temple.

Fellowship with Gentiles

In his vision, Peter has been explicitly instructed that God does not wish him to be bound by the Deuteronomic dietary laws (Acts 10:15). However, Peter senses that the implications of such a command go well beyond matters of diet and so is "perplexed as to what the vision which he had seen might mean" (Acts 10:17). While he is "pondering the vision" (Acts 10:19), the men sent by Cornelius arrive at the house, and the Holy Spirit instructs Peter to "go down, and accompany them without hesitation" (Acts 10:20). Here Peter is given a crucial clue about the meaning of the vision: As a Jew, he would not normally accompany Gentiles anywhere.

The messengers tell Peter that they have been sent to summon him to the home of the centurion Cornelius. Yet, in making their request, they are fully aware that Jews such as Peter do not visit Gentiles in their homes, and so they try to make the request more palatable by relating that Cornelius is a "God-fearing man, who is well spoken of by the whole Jewish nation" (Acts 10:22). Peter now realizes the import of his vision. Not only must he no longer consider the foods prohibited by Deuteronomy 14 to be unclean or common, but also he must no longer consider the Gentiles to be so either. This is why the Spirit had commanded him to accompany the men "without hesitation" (Acts 10:20), even to the house of a Gentile. The apostle knows that he must no longer refrain from fellowship with Gentiles such as these men, "so he called them in to be his guests" for the night (Acts 10:23).

The next day, Peter travels with the messengers and some of the disciples from Joppa to Cornelius's home in Caesarea (Acts 10:23-24). Standing in the house of a Gentile, perhaps for the first time in his life, Peter forthrightly conveys his new understanding to Cornelius's household:

> You yourselves know how unlawful it is for a Jew to associate with or to visit any one of another nation; but God has shown me that I should not call any man common or unclean. So when I was sent for, I came without objection (Acts 10:28-29).

Cornelius describes the angelic vision he received (Acts 10:30-33), and in response Peter preaches the Gospel to the household.

Good News for the Gentiles

Peter begins with a remarkable statement of the ethnic universality of the New Covenant: "Truly I perceive that God shows no partiality, but in every nation [*éthnei*] any one who fears him and does what is right is acceptable to him" (Acts 10:34-35). The criterion for acceptance by God is thus the same for those "in every nation," implying that the restored Israel is not itself a nation but international.

Peter then describes the ministry of Jesus in light of its universal significance. Though Jesus Himself worked only among Jews, His ministry was oriented from the beginning to all the nations. Hence, Jesus is the "Lord of all" (Acts 10:36). Isaiah's prophecy of liberation (cf. Is. 61:1), fulfilled by Jesus, was meant not only for the Jews but also for the Gentiles. The Jews put Jesus "to death by hanging him on a tree" (Acts 10:39), but this very act of rejection allowed Jesus to assume the Deuteronomic curse and free both Jew and Gentile to receive the Spirit apart from the Deuteronomic Law.

> Christ redeemed us from the curse of the law, having become a curse for us—for it is written, "Cursed be every one who hangs on a tree"—that in Christ Jesus the blessing of Abraham might come upon the Gentiles, that we might receive the promise of the Spirit through faith (Gal. 3:13-14).

After His Resurrection, Jesus "ate and drank" with His disciples (Acts 10:41), making Himself known to them in Eucharistic communion (cf. Lk. 24:30-31),[2] just as He would soon make Himself known to men of all nations "from east and west, and from north and south," who would come and "sit at table in the kingdom of God" (Lk. 13:29) and participate in the messianic feast. Jesus is "the one ordained by God to be judge of the living and the dead" from all nations (Acts 10:42; cf. Mt. 25:32). Thus, "every one," whether Jew or Gentile, "who believes in him receives forgiveness of sins through his name" (Acts 10:43).

Peter concludes by noting that "all the prophets bear witness" to Jesus' messianic ministry (Acts 10:43). The prophets depicted salvation as coming in two phases. First, a remnant of Israel would be restored, and then the restored Israel would draw men from all nations into herself (cf. Is. 2:2-4; 49:5-6; Zech. 8:23; 14:8-9). Jesus' earthly ministry was

---

[2] Peter Stuhlmacher, *Reconciliation, Law, and Righteousness: Essays in Biblical Theology*, trans. Everett R. Kalin (Philadelphia: Fortress Press, 1986), 56.

primarily concerned with the first phase (cf. Mt. 15:22-28), and He charged His apostles to carry out the second (cf. Acts 1:8). Now, in the last days of the Deuteronomic covenant, the Spirit has been poured out on all flesh (cf. Acts 2:17), making clean all that was unclean and thus making possible the incorporation of the Gentiles into the restored Israel. The presence and action of the Holy Spirit therefore abolishes the Pharisaic program of separation from the Gentile world. Although the Pharisees knew the prophecies of the Gentiles' entry into Israel, they had misinterpreted them to mean that the Gentiles would one day embrace the Deuteronomic covenant and its Law. The Pharisees did not imagine that God would act in a far bolder way to bring about a "new thing" (cf. Is. 43:19).

The Sovereign Spirit

Before Peter can finish speaking, the gift of the Spirit is poured out on all present, "even on the Gentiles" (Acts 10:45). The Holy Spirit visibly incorporates the Gentiles into the People of God and thereby serves as an unquestionable sign to Peter that the Gentiles must not be denied Baptism. So definitive is this sign that Peter will repeatedly appeal to it as the justification for his unprecedented actions when they later come under attack. Without hesitation, he commands the Jewish disciples to baptize Cornelius and his household (cf. Acts 10:48). In doing so, he affirms that one is brought into the New Covenant not by circumcision but by Baptism and the Holy Spirit. God is acting to fulfill His promise to bless the nations, but not within the boundaries of the Deuteronomic covenant. Peter has inaugurated the mission to the Gentiles, and he will subsequently remain active in that mission, in no way restricting his apostolate to the circumcised. After the Baptism of Cornelius and his household, Peter remains and eats with them (cf. Acts 10:48; 11:3), showing that he has not only baptized these Gentiles but also established complete fellowship with them.

Covenant Confusion

News of the conversions travels quickly to Jerusalem, and upon Peter's return to the city, he is criticized by the "circumcision party" (Acts 11:2). Luke later relates that the circumcision party consisted of Pharisees who had become disciples of Jesus while continuing to advocate strict adherence to the Deuteronomic Law (Acts 15:5). The circumcision party criticizes Peter not for preaching to Gentiles and baptizing them, but for visiting and eating with them (cf. Acts 11:3). In other words, the central issue for the circumcision party is table fellowship and its implications for the maintenance of the Deuteronomic covenant.

Defending his actions, Peter recounts the story of his encounter with Cornelius, beginning with his own vision in Joppa and concluding with the bestowal of the Holy Spirit on the Gentiles (Acts 11:5-16). The gift of the Spirit is the definitive proof that the mission to the uncircumcised, including fellowship with them, is in accordance with the will of God: "If then God gave the same gift to them as he gave to us when we believed in the Lord Jesus Christ, who was I that I could withstand God?" (Acts 11:17) The Holy Spirit both compels and legitimates the abolition of separation between the Jewish and Gentile disciples. When Peter finishes his account, his critics in the Jerusalem Church are "silenced," and "they glorified God," giving their approval to the new mission (Acts 11:18).

Mission in Antioch

Having described Peter's inauguration of the Gentile mission, Luke returns to his account of the Hellenist disciples "who were scattered because of the persecution that arose over Stephen" (Acts 11:19). The Hellenists spread the Gospel well beyond the borders of Judea and Samaria, at first "speaking the word to none except Jews" (Acts 11:19). Later, however, some of the Hellenists in Antioch began to preach also to the Gentiles (Acts 11:20). Thus, the mission in Antioch proceeded in two phases according to the prophetic pattern of evangelism that Paul would continue to employ: "to the Jew first and also to the Greek" (Rom. 1:16).

The Gentile mission in Antioch met with great success (cf. Acts 11:21), making the Church in that city the first to have a sizable number of Gentile members and resulting in a mixed congregation of Jewish and Gentile disciples. Such mixed congregations were to become the norm throughout the missionary Churches of the northeastern Mediterranean. Nowhere in Acts is there found a separate "Gentile Church." Rather, Gentiles were freely incorporated into Churches that were founded and led by Jewish disciples, Churches in which Jew and Gentile lived in communion together as one People of God.

The Ministry of Barnabas

In response to the success of the Antioch mission, the Jerusalem Church sends Barnabas to Antioch to oversee the Church there (cf. Acts 11:22). By delegating Barnabas, a trusted associate of the apostles, the Church in Jerusalem underscores the apostles' approval of the Gentile mission. After inspecting the mission, Barnabas expresses his own endorsement, and under his leadership, the Church in Antioch continues to grow rapidly (cf. Acts 11:23-24). Eventually, a point is reached at which Barnabas feels the need for an assistant to help him instruct the new disciples, and he travels to Tarsus to seek out Saul (cf. Acts 11:25). Saul had returned to his native city after fleeing from Jerusalem (cf. Acts 9:30) and evidently had remained there since that time. Barnabas enlists Saul to return with him to Antioch, where they instruct great numbers of converts (cf. Acts 11:26).

Agabus, a prophet from Jerusalem, tells the Church in Antioch of an impending "great famine" (Acts 11:28). This famine, which is also known from other historical sources, affected different areas of the Roman empire at different times; it struck Judea in the years A.D. 44-46.[3] The Antioch Church, which by this time was probably much wealthier than the Jerusalem Church, responds to the famine by taking up a collection and sending it to Jerusalem "by the hand of Barnabas and Saul" (Acts 11:30). The

---

[3] Rainer Riesner, *Paul's Early Period: Chronology, Mission Strategy, Theology*, trans. Doug Stott (Grand Rapids: William B. Eerdmans Publishing Company, 1998), 132-34.

Jerusalem Church had originally sent Barnabas to
Antioch to provide spiritual aid; the Antioch Church
now sends him back to provide material aid, indicating the continuing bond of communion between the
Churches. Luke states that Barnabas and Saul deliver
the aid to the "elders" (*presbutérous*, Acts 11:30). This
verse contains the first mention in Acts of elders or
priests (from the Greek *presbúteros*) as leaders within
the Church. The appointment of elders by the apostles and their successors began in Jerusalem and was
followed throughout the missionary Churches.

* * *

Questions for Discussion

1. Read Catechism, no. 775, about the Church as the
sacrament of the unity of the human race.

a. What obstacles rooted in his own beliefs did Peter
have to overcome in order to begin evangelizing the
Gentiles?

_____

_____

b. What obstacles do we face today in evangelizing
people who come from different nations and speak
different languages?

_____

_____

c. To what extent do we set up boundaries in our own minds about whom we share the faith with? Do we discuss the faith only with our family and friends?

_____

_____

2. The Holy Spirit is the major protagonist of Acts 10, leading the way at each step toward the incorporation of the Gentiles into Israel.

a. How do the actions of the Holy Spirit lead the disciples to an expanded definition of Israel?

_____

_____

b. How do those actions show that the Holy Spirit is sovereign over the covenants God makes with man?

_____

_____

3. Peter obeys the directions of the Holy Spirit and initiates the mission to the Gentiles.

a. To what extent do Catholics today appreciate the foundational role played by Peter in this pivotal development in salvation history?

_____

_____

b. Why is Peter's role sometimes downplayed in comparison with the subsequent work of Paul?

_____

_____

c. Read Acts 11:18. When Peter speaks, his critics in the Jerusalem Church are silenced. Do we have the proper attitude of religious assent to the decisions of the pope, who is the successor of Peter?

_____

_____

9

To the End of the Earth
—Acts 12-14—

I n Acts 12-14, Luke describes the renewal of persecution experienced by the Church in Jerusalem,
the departure of Peter from that city, and the
spread of the Gospel from Antioch to points west-
ward. The new exodus is underway, and the People
of God now carry the Gospel out of Jerusalem and
into the rest of the Roman Empire, pressing ever
closer to Rome itself.

The persecution in Jerusalem is renewed by Herod
Agrippa, the grandson of Herod the Great. Herod
Agrippa was appointed king of Judea and Samaria
by the emperor Claudius in A.D. 41, and he pursued
a strategy of currying favor with his Jewish subjects
to bolster his questionable legitimacy.[1] Persecuting
the Church was evidently a policy popular with his
subjects, and so Herod has James the Greater, the
brother of John, arrested and executed "with the
sword" (Acts 12:2). This detail is significant because it
suggests the crime with which James was charged.
Execution by sword was not the usual form of capital
punishment under the Deuteronomic Law, but was
reserved for the most heinous of offenses, most
prominently apostasy (cf. Deut. 13:12-15). Herod,
then, may have condemned James as an apostate.
However, Luke shows through the narrative of Acts 12
that the true apostates are not those Jews who have
accepted the Messiah of Israel but those who have
rejected Him. For the apostles, of course, James was

---

[1] Josephus, *Antiquities of the Jews*, bk. 19, chap. 7, no. 3.

no apostate, so when he is killed, they do not elect another to replace him, as they had in the case of Judas (cf. Acts 1:15-26). James, unlike Judas, has not disqualified himself from the apostolic college; on the contrary, he has witnessed to his office with his blood and so is not in need of replacement.

The New Exodus

When Herod sees that the execution of James is popular among his Jewish subjects, he has Peter arrested for an encore. The Passover week has begun, and Herod plans to make a spectacle of Peter's execution after the week is completed (cf. Acts 12:4). In the meantime, the chief of the apostles is held in prison, and the Church fervently intercedes for him in prayer (cf. Acts 12:5). The fact that Peter's imprisonment takes place during the Passover week recalls the Exodus, when Israel was liberated from the bondage of Egypt.[2] Through a series of allusions, Luke highlights the theme of the new exodus, in which the People of God is liberated from the Adamic and Deuteronomic curses. In the new exodus, unbelieving Jews have taken on the role of the Egyptians, with Herod acting as the new Pharaoh.

The Deliverance of Peter

At the end of the week, an "angel of the Lord" comes to Peter in prison and instructs him to "[g]et up quickly. . . . Dress yourself and put on your sandals"

---

[2] O. Wesley Allen, Jr., *The Death of Herod: The Narrative and Theological Function of Retribution in Luke-Acts*, Society of Biblical Literature Dissertation Series, no. 158, ed. E. Elizabeth Johnson (Atlanta: Scholars Press, 1997), 98.

(Acts 12:7-8), echoing the instructions given to the Israelites to eat the Passover with "your loins girded, your sandals on your feet, and . . . in haste" (Ex. 12:11) before the angel of the Lord passes through the land of Egypt. The angel leads Peter out of the prison, rescuing him "from the hand of Herod" (Acts 12:11), just as God had rescued Israel "out of the hand of the Egyptians" (Ex. 3:8).

Peter heads to the house of a prominent disciple, Mary, where many disciples have gathered to pray for him (cf. Acts 12:12). By emphasizing the Church's prayer for Peter both before and after the account of his escape, Luke suggests that the angelic intercession was in response to this prayer. Luke also relates that Mary is the mother of John, whose Roman name is Mark (cf. Acts 12:12). Mark will soon accompany his cousin Barnabas as a missionary (cf. Acts 12:25; 13:5; Col. 4:10) and will later accompany Peter (cf. 1 Pet. 5:13), on the basis of whose preaching he will compose the second Gospel. After convincing the gathered disciples of his identity (cf. Acts 12:13-16), Peter describes how the Lord "brought him out [*exégen*] of the prison" (Acts 12:17), just as He had come down to bring Israel out (*exegageîn*, Septuagint) of the land of Egypt (cf. Ex. 3:8).

Peter then departs from Jerusalem and leaves the Church in that city in the charge of James the Less (cf. Acts 12:17). Luke ends his account of Peter's escape with a description of Herod's gruesome death because of the latter's acceptance of a blasphemous acclamation of divinity. Herod refused to give "God the glory" and, like Pharaoh, was therefore struck down (Acts 12:23; cf. Ex. 14:17-18). Pagan kings, not least those of Egypt, were often worshipped as gods, and Herod was apparently not immune to this idolatrous temptation.

The narrative is now complete. As Israel escaped from Egypt while Pharaoh was judged, so Peter has escaped from Jerusalem while Herod is judged.

The Mission of Barnabas and Saul

Barnabas and Saul, who came to Jerusalem to deliver aid during the famine (cf. Acts 11:27-30), now return to Antioch, taking Mark with them (cf. Acts 12:25). Their return sets the stage for the first organized missionary journey to spread the Gospel systematically among the Gentiles (cf. Acts 13-14). Such a mission could not take place until Peter had initiated table fellowship with the Gentiles in Acts 11. The first destination selected by Barnabas and Saul is Cyprus (cf. Acts 13:4), possibly because Barnabas is a native of the island (cf. Acts 4:36). In Cyprus, they begin by proclaiming "the word of God in the synagogues of the Jews" (Acts 13:5), as would become Paul's usual practice throughout his ministry (cf. Rom. 1:16). Only when he was driven out of the local synagogues would he begin preaching in other settings.

In the city of Paphos, the new missionaries have to contend with a Jewish false prophet named Elymas, who serves as a counselor to the Roman proconsul and tries to dissuade the latter from listening to them (cf. Acts 13:7-8). Saul, however, "filled with the Holy Spirit" (Acts 13:9) and thus speaking with the authority of a true prophet, denounces Elymas, who is thereupon struck blind as a sign of the spiritual darkness in which he had tried to keep others.

Citizen of Rome

Up until Acts 13:9, Luke has consistently presented Barnabas as the senior partner in ministry with Saul. From this point forward, however, Saul becomes more prominent. Luke begins to use exclusively Saul's Roman name, Paul, reflecting Saul's own practice when dealing with Gentiles. By switching to his Roman name, Luke suggests the reason for Paul's increased prominence. Paul was a Roman citizen and possessed a Hellenistic education as well as a Pharisaic one.[3] He was thus able to move among the upper classes of Greco-Roman society, unlike many of the other disciples. The first fruit of Paul's missionary effort is the proconsul himself, who "believed" and "was astonished at the teaching of the Lord" (Acts 13:12).

The missionaries sail from Cyprus to Perga, a city on the coast of Asia Minor. Once on land, Mark departs from the group. Luke gives no reason for Mark's departure but does mention that he returned directly to Jerusalem rather than to the group's missionary base in Antioch. Mark may have had reservations about aspects of Paul's preaching to the Gentiles. In any case, it is likely that once in Jerusalem, Mark reported to the Church on the activities of the missionaries. Shortly thereafter, some disciples go from Jerusalem to Antioch to urge the Gentile converts to begin to adhere to the Deuteronomic Law (cf. Acts 15:1), and Paul later displays great anger over Mark's departure from the mission (cf. Acts 15:36-40).

---

[3] Ben Witherington III, *The Paul Quest: The Renewed Search for the Jew of Tarsus* (Downers Grove, Ill.: InterVarsity Press, 1998), 69-73, 94-98.

The Sermon at Pisidian Antioch

The missionaries travel from Perga to Pisidian Antioch, located north of Perga in the southern portion of Galatia. In Pisidian Antioch, they head for the synagogue on the next sabbath and are invited to preach by the "rulers of the synagogue" (Acts 13:15). The synagogue rulers were Jewish officials whose main responsibility was the direction of the synagogue service; they designated who would read from Scripture, recite the liturgical prayers, and give the sermon.

Thus, Paul comes to give the first major sermon of his missionary career. Luke views this sermon as a model of Paul's preaching and devotes more space to it than to any other sermon of Paul. The theme of the sermon is the "good news" (Acts 13:32) that the promises of the Davidic covenant have now been fulfilled by the Resurrection of Jesus (cf. Acts 13:23, 32-33). The sermon has strong parallels to both Peter's speech at Pentecost (cf. Acts 2:14-36) and Stephen's speech before the Sanhedrin (cf. Acts 7:2-53), showing Paul's dependence on earlier apostolic preaching. However, the sermon also broaches for the first time Paul's more developed understanding of the Deuteronomic covenant and its relation to the New Covenant (cf. Acts 13:39).

Paul begins the sermon by addressing the "[m]en of Israel" (Acts 13:16) and the Gentile God-fearers present in the synagogue, and he thereby sets the stage for his theme of the restoration of Israel scattered among the Gentiles. He then gives a summary of Israel's history and highlights God's faithfulness to His covenants. This summary follows the outline of

Stephen's sermon (cf. Acts 7:2-46) and traces the sequence of covenants from the patriarchs to David. Paul explains that God "chose our fathers" through His covenant with Abraham (Acts 13:17). The election of Israel is one of the core doctrines of the Old Testament. The doctrine is not one of ethnocentric privilege but rather explains the manner in which the Creator deals with the rebellion of His creatures. Israel was elected in order to bless and redeem the nations, a purpose that God revealed to Abraham (cf. Gen. 22:18) and began to fulfill through David.

In Acts 13:22, Paul describes David with a composite reference drawn from several Old Testament passages, beginning with Psalm 89:20: "I have found David, my servant; with my holy oil I have anointed him." Psalm 89 not only refers to God's anointing of David, but also to His covenantal oath to establish the kingdom of David's descendant (cf. Ps. 89:3-4). Thus, the psalm serves as a meditation on the promises given to David in 2 Samuel 7:12-13:

> I will raise up your offspring [spérma, Septuagint] after you, who shall come forth from your body, and I will establish his kingdom. He shall build a house for my name, and I will establish the throne of his kingdom for ever (2 Sam. 7:12-13, RSVCE and Septuagint).

Paul asserts that these promises have now been fulfilled, for "[o]f this man's posterity [spérmatos] God has brought to Israel a Savior, Jesus, as he promised" (Acts 13:23).

In Acts 13:26-31, Paul explains how the ministry of Jesus, culminating in His Resurrection, demonstrates that He is the Messiah. Those who are true sons of Abraham, including the God-fearing Gentiles, must accept the son of David as the Savior who will lead Israel to her salvation (cf. Acts 13:26). The rejection of Jesus by the Jerusalem leaders does not detract from His messianic status, but ironically confirms it, because such rejection is precisely what the Scriptures predicted (Acts 13:27; cf. 2:23). The prophets foretold the last days of the Deuteronomic covenant, which commenced when the Jerusalem leaders brought about Jesus' Passion and death. By His death on a "tree" (Acts 13:29), the son of Abraham and David has taken upon Himself the Deuteronomic curses (cf. Deut. 21:23; Gal. 3:13-16). By His Resurrection, He has demonstrated both His own victory over those curses and His power to free those who place their faith in Him (cf. Acts 13:30-31).

The Resurrection is therefore the fulfillment of the promises given to Abraham and David. Indeed, Paul sets forth this covenantal fulfillment as the definition of the Gospel: "the good news that what God promised to the fathers, this he has fulfilled to us their children by raising Jesus" (Acts 13:32-33). Paul indicates the significance of the Resurrection by quoting Psalm 2:7 ["Thou art my son, today I have begotten thee" (Acts 13:33)]. This verse echoes God's declaration about the heir of David in the covenantal formula of 2 Samuel 7:14 ("I will be his father, and he shall be my son"). Psalm 2 celebrates the royal enthronement of the heir of David. The promise given to David of a throne to be established forever (cf. 2 Sam. 7:13) is fulfilled by the enthronement of Jesus in heaven following His Resurrection and

Ascension. Psalm 2:7 therefore serves as a testimony that Jesus is the enthroned Messiah (cf. Heb. 1:5).

Paul further emphasizes the connection between the Resurrection and the Davidic covenant by paraphrasing Isaiah 55:3: "I will give you the holy and sure blessings of David" (Acts 13:34). This verse contains the most explicit reference to the Davidic covenant in the Book of Isaiah, promising to give Israel ("you" in the plural) the blessings of David in an "everlasting covenant" (Is. 55:3). The passage in Isaiah from which Acts 13:34 is drawn offers Israel the possibility of an end to the Deuteronomic curses through a restoration of the Davidic covenant. Such a restoration would involve blessings for the nations:

> Behold, I made [David] a witness to the peoples, a leader and commander for the peoples. Behold, you shall call nations that you know not, and nations that knew you not shall run to you, because of the LORD your God, and of the Holy One of Israel, for he has glorified you (Is. 55:4-5).

The condition for such covenantal restoration, however, is repentance:

> Seek the LORD while he may be found, call upon him while he is near; let the wicked forsake his way, and the unrighteous man his thoughts; let him return to the LORD, that he may have mercy on him, and to our God, for he will abundantly pardon (Is. 55:6-7).

The Resurrection represents the power of Christ to restore Israel and the nations to covenantal relation to God through repentance.

Paul underscores the centrality of the Resurrection by citing David's own words from Psalm 16:10: "Thou wilt not let thy Holy One see corruption" (Acts 13:35). Paul employs this psalm in a manner very similar to Peter in the latter's Pentecost sermon (cf. Acts 2:25-31) and argues that because David did in fact die and "see corruption," the prophecy must apply to someone else, namely the Messiah Jesus, who died but was soon raised up (cf. Acts 10:36-37).

Reaching the climax of the sermon, Paul proclaims that because Jesus has fulfilled the promises given to David, He now offers forgiveness and justification to all who believe in Him:

> [T]hrough this man forgiveness [*áphesis*] of sins is proclaimed to you, and by him every one that believes is freed [*dikaiōthênai*] from everything from which you could not be freed [*dikaioûtai*] by the law of Moses (Acts 13:38-39).

"Forgiveness" or "release" (*áphesis*) entails the lifting of the covenantal curses. To "free" or "justify" (*dikaióō*) refers to the restoration of covenantal relation with God. Clearly distinguishing the Deuteronomic covenant from the New Covenant, Paul explains that in the latter, one is justified by faith in Jesus as the Messiah, whereas the Mosaic Law does not justify at all. Speaking to an audience of both Jews and Gentiles, Paul declares that the New Covenant is open to "every one" (Acts 13:39) regardless of prior status in the Deuteronomic covenant, on the same condition of faith. By so characterizing the condition for justification, Paul has drawn out what was implicit regarding the Mosaic Law in the preaching of Peter and Stephen.

Paul closes with a prophetic warning from Habakkuk 1:5 for those Jews inclined to disbelieve and reject the Gospel (cf. Acts 13:40-41), as some will indeed do (cf. Acts 13:45). Habakkuk 1:5 concerns the impending conquest of Jerusalem by a foreign empire. In Habakkuk's day, Jerusalem was menaced by Babylon, just as in Paul's day, it is menaced by Rome. Paul's warning therefore pertains not only to eternal judgment, but also to an impending temporal judgment for those who cling to the bonds of nationality in preference to faith in Jesus.

Rejection by the Synagogue

The immediate response to the sermon is overwhelmingly positive. Barnabas and Paul are invited to return on the following sabbath to speak again, and many who hear the sermon become disciples (cf. Acts 13:42-43). However, the very success of Paul's preaching soon begins to create friction within the synagogue. On the next sabbath, a huge crowd shows up at the synagogue. Luke describes the crowd as made up of "almost the whole city" (Acts 13:44), implying that it consists mostly of Gentiles, including many who are not even God-fearers. Many of the Jews are "filled with jealousy" at the sight of the predominantly Gentile crowd (Acts 13:45). It is now evident to them that Paul's preaching of covenantal fulfillment entails an enlargement of the People of God beyond the ethnic boundaries established by the Deuteronomic Law. They reject such an understanding of God's saving action as an affront to their ethnic identity, and thus Saint Luke records that they "contradicted what was spoken by Paul, and reviled him" (Acts 13:45).

Barnabas and Paul respond by declaring that those Jews who reject the Gospel have judged themselves "unworthy of eternal life" (Acts 13:46), showing by their very opposition that they are not among the elect of Israel. Indeed, these Jews have misunderstood the election of Israel, thinking that it consists chiefly in submission to the Deuteronomic covenant through obedience to its Law. They believe that election is given first and foremost to Israel as a nation. In contrast, Paul has asserted that the election of Israel passes through the Son of David, from whom its blessings now flow to all the nations.

A Light to the Gentiles

Prevented from continuing to teach in the synagogue, Barnabas and Paul begin preaching directly to the Gentiles of Pisidian Antioch (cf. Acts 13:46) and will turn again to preach to the Jews only when they reach the next city. The missionaries explain this course of action in terms of Isaiah 49:6, which describes the mission of the servant of the Lord:

> It is too light a thing that you should be my servant to raise up the tribes of Jacob and to restore the preserved of Israel; I will give you as a light to the nations, that my salvation may reach to the end of the earth (Is. 49:6).

Isaiah's oracle refers to two divine actions: the restoration of Israel and the salvation of the Gentiles. However, because the twelve tribes (and especially the northern tribes) of Israel have been dispersed among the Gentiles, these two actions are closely linked. Indeed, the salvation of the Gentiles will be the very means by which the servant restores Israel:

> Thus says the Lord God: "Behold, I will lift up my hand to the nations, and raise my signal to the peoples; and they shall bring your sons in their bosom, and your daughters shall be carried on their shoulders (Is. 49:22).

The servant is none other than the Messiah, whose coming has now made possible the prophesied salvation and restoration, as Simeon proclaimed upon seeing the child Jesus in the Temple: "[M]ine eyes have seen thy salvation which thou hast prepared in the presence of all peoples, a light for revelation to the Gentiles, and for glory to thy people Israel" (Lk. 2:30-32). Jesus "had given commandment through the Holy Spirit to the apostles" (Acts 1:2) to advance the kingdom "in Jerusalem and in all Judea and Samaria and to the end of the earth" (Acts 1:8). Barnabas and Paul now carry on this mission. They too have been commanded through the Holy Spirit to advance the kingdom to the end of the earth (cf. Acts 13:2, 47).

The missionaries meet with success among the Gentiles of Pisidian Antioch, and "the word of the Lord spread throughout all the region" (Acts 13:49). However, the Jewish opponents of Barnabas and Paul are no more willing to allow them to preach to the Gentiles outside the synagogue than inside, and so they "stirred up persecution" against the missionaries and "drove them out of their district" (Acts 13:50). Barnabas and Paul respond by moving to their next mission field, Iconium (Acts 13:51). As consistently demonstrated in Acts, however great the suffering that opposition to the Gospel may cause the disciples, in the providence of God such opposition only serves to advance the kingdom.

*   *   *

Questions for Discussion

1. Read Acts 12:1-2 and Catechism, nos. 2473-74, about martyrdom. Prior to sending an angel to deliver Peter from the grasp of Herod, God allowed James the Greater to be martyred.

a. What is the role of martyrdom in advancing the kingdom of God?

_____

_____

b. What opportunities do we have to witness sacrificially to the Gospel in our professional and family lives?

_____

_____

2. Read Exodus 12. What are the parallels between the exodus from Egypt and the persecution of the Church in Jerusalem?

_____

_____

3. Read Acts 12:5-12 and Catechism, nos. 334-36.

a. How is the Church's prayer for Peter related to his rescue from prison by an angel?

_____

_____

b. What insight for our own prayer lives can we draw from this passage in Acts?

_____

_____

4. Paul's education was an essential factor in his ability to reach Gentile society effectively with the Gospel.

a. In what ways do we pursue the education and formation necessary to serve as credible witnesses to Christ in the settings in which He places us?

_____

_____

b. In what ways do we overly compartmentalize our "secular" and "religious" educations, failing to see the manner in which they influence and undergird each other?

_____

_____

5. Read Acts 13:32-33, where Paul defines the Gospel as God's fulfillment of His promise to raise up a son of David whose kingdom would last forever.

a. To what extent do we understand ourselves to be subjects of a kingdom higher than any earthly nation or state?

---

b. To what extent do we grasp our duty to serve that kingdom before any lesser interests?

---

6. Read Acts 7:36, 42 and 13:18; 1 Corinthians 10:1-11; and Hebrews 3:1-4:11. How do the forty years the Israelites spent in the desert with Moses parallel the forty years from the death of Jesus to the destruction of the Temple?

---

7. Read Acts 2:14-36 and 13:16-41.

a. What are the similarities between the preaching of Paul and the preaching of Peter?

---

b. What are the differences?

10

THE COUNCIL OF JERUSALEM
—ACTS 15—

The Church of Antioch was the first to have a large number of Gentile disciples (cf. Acts 11:20-21). The incompatibility of the Deuteronomic and New Covenants was first sharply experienced in the liturgical practice of that Church. Whereas the New Covenant enjoins Eucharistic communion among all disciples, Gentile or Jew, the Deuteronomic covenant prohibited such fellowship. As a result, it soon became apparent that the Deuteronomic covenant could not be preserved within the New Covenant.

Peter had previously baptized and eaten with uncircumcised Gentiles (cf. Acts 10-11), and the Jerusalem Church had ultimately given its consent to such fellowship (cf. Acts 11:18). Nevertheless, table fellowship between Jewish and Gentile disciples continued to be a source of conflict because the Jewish disciples continued to adhere to the Deuteronomic Law, according to which the uncircumcised were unclean. During the forty-year period of the last days, the Jewish disciples were permitted (though not obliged) to continue to live according to the Deuteronomic Law, which had not yet completely fallen away, as it would after the destruction of the Temple in A.D. 70.[1]

---

[1] *Cantate Domino*, Council of Florence (1442), in Henry Denzinger, *The Sources of Catholic Dogma*, 30th ed., trans. Roy J. Deferrari (St. Louis: B. Herder Book Co., 1957), no. 712; St. Thomas Aquinas, *Commentary on Saint Paul's Epistle to the Galatians*, Aquinas Scripture Series, vol. 1, trans. F. R. Larcher, O.P. (Albany: Magi Books, 1966), 49-50; St. Augustine, Letter 82, chap. II, no. 15.

This period was also marked by the rise throughout Palestine of the Zealot movement, which sought to defend Jewish nationality by means of violence. Jewish persecution of the disciples, spurred on by the Zealots, was directly linked to the presence among the disciples of uncircumcised Gentiles. Table fellowship between Jews and Gentiles, in particular, was perceived by the Zealots as a threat to their national identity. Hence, Jewish disciples who continued to adhere to the Deuteronomic Law came under great pressure to bring the Gentile disciples under that Law as well, so as to remove a target of attack for the Zealots. The "circumcision party" among the disciples (cf. Acts 11:2-3) adopted a fallback position; they asserted that while the uncircumcised could be baptized, they must subsequently be circumcised and follow the Deuteronomic Law.

This claim of the circumcision party ignites the most contentious theological conflict of the apostolic Church and leads to the Council of Jerusalem, where the issue is debated and decided. The conflict addressed at the council is not one between Gentiles and Jews. On the contrary, both the circumcision party and its strongest opponents consist of Jews. Indeed, Luke mentions not a single Gentile disciple as even being present at the council. What is in dispute at the council is not whether the Old Testament should be abandoned, but the manner in which it is being fulfilled.

Conflict in Antioch

The conflict begins when members of the circumcision party come from Judea to Antioch and begin to teach that "[u]nless you are circumcised according to the custom of Moses, you cannot be saved" (Acts 15:1). The teaching of the circumcision party is not merely that obedience to the Deuteronomic Law is a salutary custom, but that it is necessary for membership in the People of God. These Judeans have come to Antioch on their own initiative and are not authorized representatives of the Jerusalem Church (cf. Acts 15:24). By demanding changes in the practices of the Church of Antioch, they contradict the judgment of Barnabas, who had already been delegated to visit that Church and expressed his approval of its practices (cf. Acts 11:22-23). The teaching of the circumcision party causes "no small dissension" in Antioch, with Paul and Barnabas opposing its claims (Acts 15:2). Dissension (*stásis*) indicates a very sharp conflict and often has the sense of violent strife or insurrection (cf. Lk. 23:19, 25; Acts 19:40; 23:10). Realizing that the conflict cannot be resolved locally, Paul and Barnabas go with others to consult "the apostles and the elders" in Jerusalem (Acts 15:2).

The Declaration of Peter

When they arrive in Jerusalem, the issue is discussed again, with "some believers who belonged to the party of the Pharisees" insisting that "[i]t is necessary to circumcise" the Gentile disciples "and to charge them to keep the law of Moses" (Acts 15:5). The apostles and elders, along with the delegates from Antioch, formally convene to consider the matter (cf. Acts 15:6), but the issue is so contentious that "much debate" takes place before it can be resolved (Acts 15:7). Finally, Peter rises and speaks,

noting that "God made choice among you, that by
my mouth" the Gentiles were first evangelized (Acts
15:7). Moreover, it is God Himself who testifies on
behalf of the Gentile disciples by "giving them the
Holy Spirit just as he did to us" (Acts 15:8). For Peter,
the matter is decided by the visible action of the
Holy Spirit:[2] Those who have received the gift of the
Spirit are sanctified and make up the People of God.
Peter therefore declares that the Holy Spirit has
removed the binding force of Deuteronomic Law,
from which sprang the distinction between Jew and
Gentile. In place of the Deuteronomic Law, the
Spirit has blessed the Gentile disciples and
"cleansed their hearts by faith" (Acts 15:9). Far from
being unclean because of their lack of circumcision,
as under the Deuteronomic Law, the Spirit has
made even their hearts clean, which that Law could
not do. Moses himself recognized the inability of the
Deuteronomic Law to cleanse the heart and prophesied that Israel would only be restored through a new
circumcision of the heart that would enable her truly
to love God (cf. Deut. 30:1-6). Ezekiel elaborated upon
this cleansing of the heart in words that point to the
water of Baptism (Ezek. 36:25-27).

Rejecting the New Law

By refusing to follow the prophetic signs given by
the Holy Spirit, the Pharisees "make trial of God"

---

[2] Richard Bauckham, "James and the Gentiles (Acts 15.13-21)," in *History,
Literature, and Society in the Book of Acts*, ed. Ben Witherington III
(Cambridge: Cambridge University Press, 1996), 154.

(Acts 15:10), just as the rebellious Israelites had during their forty years in the wilderness (cf. Ex. 17:2; Deut. 6:16). The Pharisees put God to the test by stubbornly "putting a yoke," the Deuteronomic Law, "upon the neck of the disciples which neither our fathers nor we have been able to bear" (Acts 15:10). They implicitly refuse to accept that the Spirit has inaugurated a New Law for the New Covenant, a law that Jesus describes as easy and light (cf. Mt. 11:29-30). Peter concludes by directly responding to the initial claim of the circumcision party concerning salvation (cf. Acts 15:1), declaring that "we shall be saved through the grace of the Lord Jesus, just as they [the Gentiles] will" (Acts 15:11). The grace of the Messiah is the only means of salvation, whether for the Jews to whom Peter had first preached during his Pentecost sermon (cf. Acts 2:21, 40) or for the Gentiles. There is thus no need for the Gentiles to come under the Deuteronomic Law.

Peter has provided the decisive judgment for the council and dispensed the Gentiles from the Deuteronomic Law as a whole. Though the council does not expressly address the question of continued adherence to the Deuteronomic Law by Jewish disciples, Peter's judgment has a clear implication for that question as well: The Deuteronomic Law is henceforth in no way necessary for membership in the People of God. At the end of Peter's speech, "all the assembly," including the Pharisees, "kept silence" (Acts 15:12). Peter's declaration ends the dispute, and from this point forward in the deliberations, no one advocates the position of the circumcision party.

A People for His Name

Barnabas and Paul then describe "what signs and wonders God had done through them among the Gentiles" (Acts 15:12). By summarizing their testimony in this manner, Luke echoes Peter's description in his Pentecost sermon of Jesus as having come with "wonders and signs which God did through him in your midst" (Acts 2:22). Through this echo, Luke suggests that the Gentiles are now in the midst of the restored Israel, a theme that will be taken up by James. The mission to the Gentiles is thus the culmination of the mission of the Messiah.

Last of all, James speaks (cf. Acts 15:13). James has been the leader of the Jerusalem Church since Peter's departure from the city (cf. Acts 12:17). Because he was a man who was devoutly obedient to the Deuteronomic Law, his word carried much weight with the Jewish disciples. He immediately refers to Peter's description of "how God first visited the Gentiles" (Acts 15:14). The notion of visitation pertains to God's intervention in salvation history (cf. 1 Pet. 2:12). James therefore interprets the gift of the Holy Spirit to the Gentiles as a divine intervention that brings the Gentiles into the People of God. Indeed, God has chosen "to take out of them a people for his name" (Acts 15:14), indicating the divine election of the Gentile remnant for covenantal status (cf. 1 Pet. 2:9-10). James' reference to Gentiles within the People of God signals the fulfillment of Zechariah 2:11: "And many nations shall join themselves to the LORD in that day, and shall be my people."

In order to show that charism and revelation are in agreement on the question at hand, James then provides the scriptural warrant for Peter's decision. The election of the Gentile remnant is an occurrence with which "the words of the prophets agree" (Acts 15:15). James refers to the prophets in the plural because he is going to give a composite chain of quotations from prophetic passages that describe the restoration of Israel (Jer. 12:15; Amos 9:11-12; Is. 45:21). Composite citation in such a style was traditional in first-century Judaism.

Building the New Temple

The opening line of this composite chain, "After this [*metà taûta*] I will return [*anastrépsō*]" (Acts 15:16), echoes two passages from the prophets concerning covenant restoration. The first describes Israel's return from exile during the last days:

> For the children of Israel shall dwell many days without king. . . . Afterward [*metà taûta*, Septuagint] the children of Israel shall return and seek the LORD their God, and David their king; and they shall come in fear to the LORD and to his goodness in the latter days (Hos. 3:4-5).

The second relates how God will gather the Gentile remnant in the midst of His holy people:

> And after I have plucked [the Gentiles] up, I will again have compassion on them, and I will bring them again [*epistrépsō*, Septuagint]. . . . And it shall come to pass, if they will diligently learn the ways of my people, to swear by my name, . . . then they shall be built up in the midst of my people (Jer. 12:15-16).

The imagery of the Gentiles being built up like a building in the midst of Israel suggests their incorporation into the new temple, the Body of Christ. Drawing on this imagery, James considers the gathering of the Gentiles in the midst of Israel to be the key to interpreting the Scriptures concerning the Gentile disciples during the last days.

James next begins a more lengthy quotation of Amos 9:11-12, which is part of an oracle of the scattering of the ten northern tribes of Israel. When Amos wrote in 760 B.C., the southern kingdom of Judah had not yet fallen. Nevertheless, Amos foretells a restoration of the kingdom of David: "I will rebuild the dwelling [*skēnēn*] of David, which has fallen; I will rebuild its ruins" (Acts 15:16; cf. Amos 9:11). The word "dwelling" (*skēnē*) is used in the Septuagint for the tabernacle and God's dwelling therein (cf. Ex. 25:9, Septuagint). Because the tabernacle was incorporated into Solomon's Temple (cf. 1 Kings 8:3-6), the term *skēnē* is also used of the latter by extension (e.g., Tobit 13:10, Septuagint). Constructed by the son of David, the Temple was uniquely associated with the house or dynasty of David (cf. 2 Sam. 7:12-13). Thus, when Amos writes that God will rebuild the *skēnē* of David, James interprets this rebuilding with reference to the new temple made up of all those united to the Messiah within the restored kingdom of David. A messianic understanding of Amos 9:11 was prevalent within first century Judaism; the Targum (or Aramaic paraphrase) to Amos 9:11, for example, reads, "At that time I will reestablish the fallen kingdom of David."[3]

---

[3] Craig A. Evans and James A. Sanders, *Luke and Scripture: The Function of Sacred Tradition in Luke-Acts* (Minneapolis: Fortress Press, 1993), 207-8.

However, the apostles teach more distinctly that the Davidic restoration has been inaugurated by Jesus' Ascension to the throne of David, as Peter explains in his Pentecost sermon (cf. Acts 2:30, 34).

The Kingdom of David

Because the fulfillment of God's promises to David has begun, "the rest of men," until now outside of Israel, "may seek the Lord" (Acts 15:17). The restored kingdom of David is thus made up not only of the twelve tribes but also of the "many people and strong nations [that] . . . seek the LORD," as the prophet Zechariah had foretold (Zech. 8:22). From these peoples and nations will be drawn "the Gentiles who are called by my name" (Acts 15:17). In the Old Testament, to be called by the name of the Lord indicates covenantal relation with God through divine election. For Amos to refer to Gentiles "who are called by my name" implies that God has elected the Gentiles to enter into covenantal relation with Himself.

By his citation of Amos 9:11-12, James indicates that the restored kingdom of David consists of a remnant of both the twelve tribes of Israel and the Gentiles, united as one People of God. Whereas the Deuteronomic covenant was national in character, the Davidic covenant was always intended to be international. Hence, the incorporation of the Gentiles apart from the Deuteronomic Law is the very means by which Jesus will "restore the kingdom to Israel" (Acts 1:6), as He suggested when He commanded the apostles to serve as His witnesses "to the end of the earth" (Acts 1:8). James completes his composite chain by saying that the Lord "has made these things known from of old" (Acts 15:18), an allusion to Isaiah 45:20-22. The latter passage concerns the remnant of the Gentiles being drawn to God in the last days:

> Assemble yourselves and come, draw near together, you survivors of the nations! . . . Who told this long ago? Who declared it of old? Was it not I, the LORD? . . . Turn to me and be saved, all the ends of the earth! (Is. 45:20-22)

The collective message of the various prophetic texts that James alludes to or quotes is that in the last days, when the kingdom of David is restored by the Messiah, God will build a new temple in which the Gentiles may dwell with Him. According to the teaching of the apostles, the new temple is the Church (cf. 1 Pet. 2:4-10; 2 Cor. 6:16; Eph. 2:19-22). The Gentiles can therefore be brought into the People of God without submitting to the Deuteronomic Law (cf. Acts 15:19).

The Apostolic Decree

Nevertheless, James immediately proposes a decree for Gentile believers that contains four prohibitions that seem to be derived from the Mosaic Law (cf. Acts 15:20). In the words of the final decree, the Gentiles should "abstain from what has been sacrificed to idols and from blood and from what is strangled and from unchastity" (Acts 15:29). James' willingness to draw upon the Mosaic Law even as he acknowledges its lack of binding force stems from the peculiar status of that Law during the forty-year period of the last days. This period constituted a transitional phase of overlap between the Deuteronomic covenant and the New Covenant. During this transitional phase, the Mosaic Law was no longer binding but had not yet been externally removed by the destruction of the Temple.

The apostolic decree represents the mandate of the Mosaic Law for those not within the Deuteronomic covenant during the last days. The decree is therefore temporary, enduring only until the destruction of the Temple in A.D. 70. The four prohibitions are characterized as "necessary things" (Acts 15:28), necessary not for salvation but nevertheless mandated by Scripture for Gentiles during this period. The decree exemplifies the manner in which the Mosaic Law points beyond itself to the New Covenant. James does not improvise the four prohibitions in an ad hoc manner, but selects them according to a particular covenantal logic from the Mosaic Law, which was proclaimed in the synagogues in every city for centuries (cf. Acts 15:21).

The prophetic texts invoked by James in Acts 15:16 pertain to Gentile believers whom Jeremiah 12:16 describes as "in the midst" of the People of God. James employs the latter phrase in a linking exegesis to identify a portion of the Mosaic Law that also relates to such Gentiles. The Mosaic Law contains many prohibitions relating to the conduct of Gentiles living in the land of Israel, but only Leviticus 17-18 contains precepts that pertain specifically to Gentiles living "in your midst." The qualification "in your midst" is not merely geographic but also communal, and James applies it to the Gentile disciples of his own day.

In the Greek version of Leviticus 17-18, the idea of the foreigner who sojourns in the midst of Israel appears five times (cf. Lev. 17:8, 10, 12, 13; 18:26) in association with prohibitions. Two of the five occurrences (cf. Lev. 17:10, 12) give the same prohibition, leaving four distinct prohibitions. These are the precepts that James considers applicable to the Gentile disciples during the last days, and thus they correspond point by point with the prohibitions given in the apostolic decree (cf. Acts 15:29). They are:

1. Improper sacrifices (cf. Lev. 17:8-9)
2. The consumption of blood (cf. Lev. 17:10-12)
3. The consumption of animals not properly slaughtered (cf. Lev. 17:13)
4. Sexual immorality (cf. Lev. 18:26, referring back to Leviticus 18:6-23)

These four prohibitions do not come close to covering the Deuteronomic dietary laws. For example, there is no mention of unclean animals, such as swine, and thus Gentiles disciples who obey the apostolic decree would still be considered unclean according to the Deuteronomic Law. The Gentile disciples are clearly not being given a partial version of the Deuteronomic Law as a pragmatic compromise with the circumcision party. Rather, the apostolic decree addresses a spiritual concern (the separation of the Gentiles from idolatry) distinct from any continuation of the Deuteronomic covenant. The four prohibitions James has drawn from Leviticus 17-18 are collectively concerned with the avoidance of idolatry (cf. Lev. 17:7), originally in its Egyptian and

Canaanite forms (cf. Lev. 18:3, 24),[4] but now applied to the paganism of the first century.

The decree is sent to "the Gentiles in Antioch and Syria and Cilicia" in the name of "the apostles and the elders" in Jerusalem (Acts 15:23), and it expressly condemns the actions of the circumcision party (cf. Acts 15:24). Meeting in a council presided over by Peter, the Church formally exercises her authority to interpret the Scriptures to decide a matter of doctrine. Hence, the apostles describe their decision as having been guided by the Holy Spirit (cf. Acts 15:28). A delegation from Jerusalem accompanies Paul and Barnabas back to Antioch to present the decree, which is received there with joy (cf. Acts 15:22, 30-31). Paul then proceeds to the churches of Syria and Cilicia (cf. Acts 15:41), delivering "for observance the decisions [dógmata] which had been reached by the apostles and elders who were at Jerusalem" (Acts 16:4). To assure the Church's survival and growth after Jerusalem falls, Paul continues with his missionary journeys in order to plant the Church securely among the Gentiles before Jerusalem is destroyed. The Church has been born, but she is still attached by the umbilical cord to the womb of Jerusalem, and that cord will soon be cut.

The People of God has undergone a transition of covenants and thus of covenantal laws, from the Deuteronomic Law to the New Law of the Spirit. The circumcision party grasped the implication of this transition and resisted it. If members of the People of

---

[4] John H. Sailhamer, *The Pentateuch as Narrative: A Biblical-Theological Commentary* (Grand Rapids: Zondervan Publishing House, 1992), 343-47.

God could remain outside the Deuteronomic Law, then the Deuteronomic covenant and the national boundaries that it upheld were no more. Thus, the apostolic decree clearly signaled that the People of God could no longer be identified with a single nation, but would henceforth embrace all nations. The judgment of Jerusalem would complete the transition of covenants, replacing the Temple made by human hands with the new temple of the Holy Spirit.

*   *   *

Questions for Discussion

1. Read Acts 15:12. After Peter has given his judgment at the Council of Jerusalem, "all the assembly kept silence," including those who had espoused an opposing view.

a. To what extent do we take seriously our obligation to submit to the teaching of the Magisterium?

_____

_____

b. Do we fail in any way to trust the Holy Spirit to guide the Church in her authoritative teaching?

_____

_____

2. Read Acts 15:17; Deuteronomy 28:10; 2 Chronicles 7:14; Jeremiah 14:9; and Daniel 9:19.

a. Summarize the meaning of being called by the name of the Lord.

_____

_____

b. As Christians, how do we live out our covenantal relation with God?

_____

_____

3. Read Acts 15:15-18. James drew upon Scripture to understand the action of the Holy Spirit in building up the Church. How can we follow a scriptural pattern when we consider and respond to the challenges that the Church faces today?

_____

_____

4. Read Catechism, nos. 81-82, 113. At the Council of Jerusalem, the Church authoritatively interpreted Scripture in order to settle a crucial doctrinal question. The circumcision party knew Scripture well but had been interpreting it in the manner of the Pharisees.

a. What does the Council of Jerusalem tell us about the relationship between Tradition and Scripture?

_____

_____

b. Can Scripture be correctly interpreted apart from the apostolic Tradition?

_____